Joe Paterno Hastily Tried Unjustly Convicted

William Rita

*To the young men who chose to play football
for Joe Paterno and stayed true to the University
he had devoted his life to. They are Penn State!*

About the Author

Mr. Rita began his career as an auditor with the U. S. Federal government's General Accounting Office, now known as the Government Accountability Office (GAO). As a certified public accountant, he spent ten years auditing and investigating federal activities and drafting reports to Congress and Congressional Committees. He served as assistant director for special audits and investigations at the General Services Administration (GSA). Later he became director of finance at that agency. In that capacity he was once quoted in a Congressional Committee report as writing that auditors "are the people who ride down from the hills after the battle and shoot the wounded."

Mr. Rita is a graduate of the University of Connecticut.

His book, *The Just Pride of Patriotism: Great Words from American History presented in the Context of the Events that Inspired them 1607–1857*, is available on amazon.com

Photo credits
Photos of Paterno victories; William Rita
Photo of family and Nittany Lion; Shirley Rita
Photo of Joe Paterno and John Rita; Chris Bartnik

Table of Contents

Penn State Beats Bowling Green, September 12, 1998

Who you going to believe The NCAA or your lying eyes?

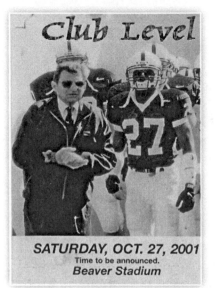

Penn State Beats Ohio State

John Batista Rita, Jay Fasick, John George Rita

Joe Paterno and John Rita in happier times

Prologue

On the day before Penn State's first game under new head coach Bill O'Brien, the following ran in the *Centre Daily Times:*
"WE ARE...

Dear Penn State Board of Trustees,

It is apparent you want us, the Alumni, to move forward. You implore us to move forward. Here is a simple fact. We can and will move forward, and will join you on a united front, if one of two things occurs. We will move forward if:

1) Indisputable evidence surfaces that clearly shows Joe Paterno knew that Jerry Sandusky was molesting boys since 1998/2001 and did nothing to stop him (it is evident that the findings of your $6.5 million Freeh report were not factually derived: www.emf.intherought.net/pennstate.htm), or

2) You admit your hasty decisions starting back in November 2011 (including firing Joe Paterno, accepting the Freeh Report, and agreeing to the NCAA sanctions) were a mistake made under pressure and not based on truth, and that, most importantly, you did not act in the best interest of Penn State University.

One day you will have to look in the mirror and admit that you allowed this debacle to spin out of control. In November 2011, Penn State had no crisis management in place, so the media naturally turned to Joe, the face of Penn State, but he was allowed to say very little. The media applied pressure; and once you, the Board, fired Joe, that was all the world needed to conclude that he must have been guilty of a cover-up. You, the Trustees, were distancing yourselves from anyone the media labeled as "guilty" so you could come out smelling like roses. Then you hired Freeh to validate your findings of Joe and again to make yourself look like the good guys. Did it not once occur to you that, by making the icon of your own University take the fall with no evidence of wrongdoing, you were potentially destroying the university? (NCAA sanctions, economic suicide, lawsuits, accreditation fallout) it seems you were anxious for so long to get rid of Joe that you could not wait to throw the last jab. And here you are reaping what you sowed.

There will never be unity between the Alumni and the Board until you start admitting your mistakes or until all of you who were active in November '11 vacate your positions, which could be years from now. You want to move on because it is too painful for you to live in this mess you made. I wonder how many of you, with the benefit of hindsight, would have done things differently the night of November 9, 2011. I'm sure it is difficult for some of you to look in the mirror or even get out of bed in the morning. We all know when we offend or do wrong to another, there are simply two choices; (wo)man up, admit our mistakes, make amends, and then move on, or sweep it under the rug and never move on. The one who was wronged can never move on until the offense is reconciled. This is why we, the alumni, cannot and will not move on.

And now you find yourselves desperate to repair and rebuild the image of Penn State, an image which you single-handedly allowed to be torn apart. Perhaps your first course of action should be to repair and rebuild the trust within our family, and then together, we can restore the image of our great university. It is time to fight for what is right. It is time to be the leaders we have entrusted you to be. Please remember this "a house divided against itself cannot stand."

Sincerely,

Eileen Morgan, Fellow Concerned Alumni,
and Friends of PSU
...PENN STATE"

Introduction

I like stories with heroes. Unfortunately, this story has none. We have the sordid tale of a pedophile, who was on the loose for years. We have a graduate assistant, police, prosecutors, welfare workers, officials at a charity for children, Penn State officials, and janitors missing a chance to bring him to justice. Unfortunately, the long, tortuous road that finally ended in Jerry Sandusky being imprisoned for his crimes created another victim.

Sexual child abuse is a political crime. By that I mean in this country, like real political crimes in dictatorships, the charge is equal to the conviction. There have been exceptions to this rule, but very few.

Jerry Sandusky was found to be a pedophile. Joe Paterno was declared the chief villain in Sandusky's continued child molestations.

Unlike the graduate assistant or the janitors, Paterno witnessed nothing. Unlike the police, prosecutors, welfare workers, and charity officials, Paterno's position gave him no direct access to details of Sandusky's activities. And unlike them, he had no professional duty to fully investigate questionable activities by Sandusky. He had less organizational responsibility than those above him at Penn State.

But Paterno alone among the participants had been honored with a statute. He alone had achieved unparalleled success in his profession. And he alone would excite the sanctimonious press.

William Buckley once quoted Professor James Burnham: "Over whatever subject, plan or issue Mrs. Roosevelt touches, she spreads a squidlike ink of directionless feeling. All distinctions are blurred, all analysis fouled, and in the murk clear thought is forever impossible."

The same can be said of the Sandusky–Penn State scandal. Press hysteria has blurred all distinctions, has made clear thought impossible.

The Sandusky tragedy made no heroes, but it destroyed the reputation of an American sports icon. Joe Paterno represented the best in big-time college football. His players were true student-athletes. His ethics insured recruiting practices that always stayed within the rules.

Through his website, FramingPaterno.com., John Ziegler has been working to restore Paterno's reputation. He recently commissioned a poll by respected pollsters. They found that 45 percent of those polled thought Paterno may have been accused of child molestation. Twenty-eight percent were sure he was. The respondents were wrong more than right on seven of eight straightforward true-or-false questions about the scandal.

In this slim volume, I am joining Eileen Morgan, John Ziegler, and many others in trying to restore the reputation of Coach Joe Paterno by bringing some clear thought to the Sandusky scandal.

William J. Rita
Springfield, VA

1

The NCAA Strikes

On July 23, 2012, the National Collegiate Athletic Association imposed sanctions on the Pennsylvania State University—sanctions that have greatly damaged its fabled football program. In eleven days the football program had been tried, convicted, and sentenced. It was a strange trial. Ex-FBI Director Louis Freeh, who had been retained by the Penn State Board of Trustees to conduct an investigation, became prosecutor. The NCAA, with no apparent authority, appointed itself judge and jury. The prosecutor had an easy task. He didn't have to cite any laws that had been broken by the football program and therefore didn't have to prove any elements of a crime. He had thousands of records, but he didn't have to turn exculpatory evidence over to the defense—always a dicey business. Did I mention there was no one to speak for the defense? Freeh didn't have to worry about losing on appeal. There was no appellate court.[1] Unlike an American corporation, the football program had no Bill of Rights protection. In 1988 the

---

[1] Seven days after the Freeh report was released and lauded, the Associated Press reported that a lifetime ban of Mohammad bin Hamman by the International Federation of Association Football had been overturned by the Court of Arbitration for Sport. The ban had been based on conclusions presented in a report by the Freeh group. The Court did not conclude bin Hamman was innocent, but it did conclude the report's evidence did not support the report's conclusions

1

Supreme Court had ruled that because the NCAA was not a "state actor," it did not have to employ due process in its proceedings. The *Washington Post* said in an editorial, "[T]he NCAA's punishment of the Penn State football program, announced Monday broke all the rules. That's good." Good indeed.

2

Grooming

My young grandson, Jay Fasick, is in the swimming pool of a Tampa hotel. Penn State is going to play Kentucky tomorrow in the 1999 Outback Bowl. Also in the pool is Penn State defensive coordinator, Jerry Sandusky, in a circle with a number of football players and young boys trying to keep a beach ball in the air. Sandusky motions for Jay to join, and he happily does. Men and boys are having a good time with the bouncing ball. I think it's kind of goofy, seeing a football coach playing this silly game. I also think this guy is incredibly nice.

Years later, Franco Harris, the great Penn State—and, later, Pittsburgh Steelers—running back, offered a perceptive comment on Sandusky, who by then was a convicted pedophile. On the Dan Patrick TV show, Harris said of Sandusky, who was always seen around kids, "Not only did he groom kids, he ultimately groomed a community." And so he did.

3

The Grand Jury

In November 2011, a Pennsylvania Grand Jury indicted Sandusky on multiple charges of sexual assaults. Charges are presented on behalf of eight victims. Much detail is given in the presentment, but we are not told the dates each victim came to the attention of the authorities; and in all but two cases, we are not told how the authorities learned of the victims.

Victim 1

The presentment states:

> During the course of the multi-year investigation, the Grand Jury heard evidence that Sandusky indecently fondled Victim 1 on a number of occasions, performed oral sex on Victim 1 on a number of occasions and had Victim 1 perform oral sex on him on at least one occasion.

According to the victim, the assaults began in 2005 or 2006, when he was eleven or twelve, and continued through 2008. Many of the assaults took place at the Sandusky residence. Sandusky took the boy to various events, including a Philadelphia Eagles game, and often gave him expensive gifts.

According to the presentment, after the boy entered high school:

> Sandusky routinely had contact with him at a Clinton County high school where the administration would call Victim 1 out of activity period/study/hall in the late afternoon to meet with Sandusky in a conference room. No one monitored these visits. Sandusky assisted the school with coaching varsity football and had unfettered access to the school.

A wrestling coach saw Sandusky and Victim 1 "wrestling" one evening in the school weight room. The coach thought it odd but apparently did or said nothing. An assistant principal said Sandusky often called youths under the care of his charity from their classrooms. He became suspicious.

The mother of Victim 1 called the school and reported a sexual assault on her son. The school called the authorities. This apparently was the beginning of an investigation. It is hard to understand how, after hearing Victim 1's story, it took three years to indict Sandusky.

Victim 2

The story of Victim 2 became the story that doomed Penn State. Here are the opening two paragraphs of the presentment related to this victim:

> On March 1, 2002, a Penn State graduate assistant ("graduate assistant") who was then 28 years old, entered the locker room at the Lasch Football Building on the University Park Campus on a Friday night before the beginning of Spring Break. The graduate assistant, who was familiar with Sandusky, was going to put some newly purchased sneakers in his locker and get some recruiting tapes to watch. It was about 9:30 p.m. As the graduate assistant entered the locker room doors, he was surprised to find the lights and showers on. He then heard rhythmic, slapping sounds. He believed the sounds to be those of sexual activity. As the graduate assistant put the

6

sneakers in his locker, he looked into the shower. He saw a naked boy, Victim 2, whose age he estimated to be ten years old, with his hands up against the wall being subjected to anal intercourse by a naked Sandusky. The graduate assistant was shocked but noticed that both Victim 2 and Sandusky saw him. The graduate assistant left immediately, distraught.

The graduate assistant went to his office and called his father, reporting to him what he had seen. His father told the graduate assistant to leave the building and come to his home. The graduate assistant and his father decided that the graduate assistant had to promptly report what he had seen to Coach Joe Paterno ("Paterno"), head football coach of Penn State. The next morning, a Saturday, the graduate assistant telephoned Paterno and went to Paterno's home where he reported what he had seen.

<u>Time out:</u> Let's imagine the conversation between the graduate assistant and his father

Graduate Assistant: Dad, I just saw Sandusky raping a kid in the shower. They were naked. The kid was up against the wall. It was horrible. What the hell do I do?
Father: Why, son, that's easy. First thing tomorrow you call Joe Paterno.

Did no one notice the absurdity of what the prosecutors are asking us to believe? If paragraph 2 is correct, paragraph 1 is virtually impossible. And notice what the prosecutors say the graduate assistant told Paterno—they say "he reported what he had seen." They have no testimony to support that assertion. The prosecutors omit the fact that the graduate assistant also told a friend of the family, a medical doctor. Maybe they thought we would believe that two men ignored a reported rape, but would not believe that three had.

The presentment continues:

> Joseph V. Paterno testified to receiving the graduate assistant's report at his home on a Saturday morning.

Paterno testified that the graduate assistant was very upset. Paterno called Tim Curley ("Curley"), Penn State Athletic Director and Paterno's immediate superior, to his home the very next day, a Sunday, and reported to him that the graduate assistant had seen Jerry Sandusky in the Lasch Building showers fondling or doing something of a sexual nature to a young boy.

<u>Time out:</u> In his Grand "Jury testimony, an eighty-four-year-old Paterno used the terms "fondling" and "sexual." His testimony will be examined in a later section. But here I want to note the prosecutor did not ask Paterno what he told Curley. Instead, he asked the leading question: "Was the information that you passed along substantially the same as the information Mr. McQueary had given you?" Paterno answered "Yes." It would have been far more informative if Paterno had been asked to describe what he told had Curley. The prosecutor probably knew what I suspect— Paterno didn't really remember what he had been told, or what he told others, ten years earlier.

The presentment continues:

Approximately one and a half weeks later, the graduate assistant was called to a meeting with Penn State Athletic Director Curley and Senior Vice President for Finance and Business Gary Schultz ("Schultz"). The graduate assistant reported to Curley and Schultz that he had witnessed what he believed to be Sandusky having anal sex with a boy in the Lasch Building showers. Curley and Schultz assured the graduate assistant that they would look into it and determine what further action they would take. Paterno was not present for this meeting.

The graduate assistant heard back from Curley a couple of weeks later. He was told that Sandusky's keys to the locker room were taken away and that the incident had been reported to The Second Mile. The graduate assistant was never questioned by University Police and no other entity conducted an investigation until he testified in

Grand Jury in December, 2010. The Grand Jury finds the graduate assistant's testimony to be extremely credible.

<u>Time out:</u> If McQueary really told the men he had seen anal sex, what in the world was there to look into? If McQueary had really reported a rape, didn't he find it a little odd that the action was to take away Sandusky's keys? Ah, yes, that should do it. The prosecutor's scenario for Victim 2 simply doesn't ring true, except to the Grand Jury members who found it "extremely credible." Credible? No, "extremely credible." This Grand Jury had read McQueary's testimony but had not heard it. McQueary had testified to an earlier group of jurors. Without seeing or hearing the witness, "extremely credible" is hardly credible.

Back to the presentment:

Curley testified that the graduate assistant reported to them that "inappropriate conduct" or activity that made him "uncomfortable" occurred in the Lasch Building shower in March 2002. Curley specifically denied that the graduate assistant reported anal sex or anything of a sexual nature whatsoever and termed the conduct as merely "horsing around." When asked whether the graduate assistant had reported "sexual conduct" "of any kind" by Sandusky, Curley answered, "No" twice. When asked if the graduate assistant had reported "anal sex between Jerry Sandusky and this child" Curley testified, "Absolutely not."

Curley testified that he informed Dr. Jack Raykovitz, executive director of the Second Mile of the conduct reported to him and met with Sandusky to advise Sandusky that he was prohibited from bringing youth onto the Penn State campus from that point forward. Curley testified that he met again with the graduate asistant and advised him that Sandusky had been directed not to use Penn State's athletic facilities with young people and "the information" had been given to director of The Second Mile. Curley testified that he also advised Penn State University President Graham Spanier of the information he had received from the graduate assistant and the steps he had taken as a result. Curley was not specific about the language he used in reporting the 2002 incident to Spanier. Spanier testified to his approval of the approach taken by Curley. Curley did not report the incident to the university police, the police agency for the University Park campus or any other police agency.

Schultz testified that he was called to a meeting with Joe Paterno and Tim Curley, in which Paterno reported "disturbing" and "inappropriate" conduct in the shower by Sandusky upon a young boy, as reported to him by a student or graduate student. Schultz was present in a subsequent meeting with Curley when the graduate assistant reported the incident in the shower involving Sandusky and a boy. Schultz was very unsure about what he remembered the graduate assistant telling him and Curley about the shower incident. He testified that he had the impression that Sandusky might have inappropriately grabbed the young boy's genitals while wrestling and agreed that such was inappropriate sexual conduct between a man and a boy. While equivocating on the definition of "sexual" in the context of Sandusky's wrestling with and grabbing the genitals of the boy, Schultz conceded that the report the graduate assistant made was of inappropriate sexual conduct by Sandusky. However Schultz testified that the allegations were "not that serious" and that he and Curley had no indication that a crime had occurred. Schultz agreed that sodomy between Sandusky and a child would clearly be inappropriate sexual conduct. He denied having such conduct reported to him either by Paterno or the graduate assistant.

Schultz testified that he and Curley agreed that Sandusky was to be told not to bring any Second Mile children into the football building and he believed that he and Curley asked "the child protection agency" to look into the matter. Schultz testified that he knew about an investigation of Sandusky that occurred in 1998, that the "child protection agency" had done, and he believed the same agency was investigating the 2002 report by the graduate assistant. Schultz acknowledged that there were similarities between the 1998 and 2002 allegations, both of which involved minor boys in the football showers with Sandusky behaving in a sexually inappropriate manner. Schultz testified that the 1998 incident was reviewed by the University police and the "child protection agency" with the blessing of then-University counsel Wendell Courtney. Courtney was and remains counsel for The Second Mile. Schultz confirmed that University President Graham Spanier was apprised in 2002 that a report of an incident involving Sandusky and a child in the shower on the campus had been reported by an employee. Schultz testified that Spanier approved the decision to ban Sandusky from bringing children into the football locker room and the decision to advise The Second Mile of the 2002 incident.

The presentment continues with discussions of Schultz's duties, Spanier's testimony, Sandusky's status at Penn State, and reporting requirements of child abuse that were allegedly violated.

The grand jury found that "portions of the testimony of Tim Curley and Gary Schultz are not credible" and that each had "made a materially false statement under oath"—Curley for claiming he "was not told by the graduate assistant that Sandusky was engaged in sexual conduct or anal sex with a boy" and Schultz for testifying that the allegations made by the graduate assistant were "not that serious" and that he and Curley "had no indication that a crime had occurred." The grand jury also concluded that "the failure to report is violation of the law...."

Victim 3
In describing the assaults against Victim 3, the presentment mentions tickling and hugging and also touching of the genitals. The events took place at a gym and Sandusky's residence, apparently beginning in 2000.

Victim 4

The presentment states this victim "was repeatedly subjected to Involuntary Deviate Sexual intercourse and Indecent assault at a number of locations including Penn State University Park campus." Oral sex was described, and "Sandusky also attempted to penetrate Victim 4's anus with both a finger and his penis. There was slight penetration and Victim 4 resisted."

Of the eight victims, only this testimony and that attributed to McQueary mention anal sex. The indictment states Sandusky gave Victim 4 many gifts, and the boy went to bowl games with the Sandusky family, including "the 1998 Outback Bowl and the 1999 Alamo Bowl."

Victim 5

This victim went to many football games and tailgate parties with Sandusky, starting about 1998. Apparently conduct with this boy didn't go beyond inappropriate touching, but there was a very disturbing incident when Sandusky "took Victim 5's hand and placed it on his erect penis." According to the victim, after rejecting Sandusky's advances, he was never again invited to football games.

Victim 6

Victim 6 was taken to a Penn State locker room in 1998, when he was eleven years old. On the drive, Sandusky put his hand on the boy's thigh several times. In the locker room they lifted weights, played with a ball, wrestled, and then showered. According to the presentment:

> Sandusky bear-hugged the boy, from behind, holding the boy's back against his chest. Then he picked him up and put him under the showerhead to rinse soap out of his hair. Victim 6 testified that the entire shower episode felt very awkward.

The presentment related to Victim 6 continues:

> When Victim 6 was dropped off at home, his hair was wet and his mother immediately questioned him

about this and was upset to learn the boy had showered with Sandusky. She reported the incident to University Police who investigated. After a lengthy investigation by University Police Detective Ronald Schreffler, the investigation was closed after then–Centre Country District Attorney Ray Gricar decided there would be no criminal charges. Schreffler testified that he was told to close the investigation by the director of the campus police, Thomas Harmon. The investigation included a second child, B. K., also 11, who was subjected to nearly identical treatment in the shower as Victim 6, according to Detective Schreffler.

Detective Schreffler testified that he and State College Police department Detective Ralph Ralston, with the consent of the mother of Victim 6, eavesdropped on two conversations the mother of Victim 6 had with Sandusky on May 13, 1998, and May 19, 1998. The mother of Victim 6 confronted Sandusky about showering with her son, the effect it had on her son, whether Sandusky had sexual feelings when he hugged her naked son in the shower and where Victim 6's buttocks were when Sandusky hugged him. Sandusky said he had showered with other boys and Victim 6's mother tried to make Sandusky promise never to shower with a boy again but he would not. She asked him if his "private parts" touched Victim 6 when he bear-hugged him. Sandusky replied, "I don't think so... maybe." At the conclusion of the second conversation, after Sandusky was told he could not see Victim 6 anymore, Sandusky said, "I understand I was wrong. I wish I could get forgiveness. I know I won't get it from you. I wish I was dead." Detective Ralston and the mother of Victim 6 confirm these conversations.

Jerry Lauro, an investigator with the Pennsylvania Department of Public Welfare, testified that during the 1998 investigation, Sandusky was interviewed on June 1, 1998, by Lauro and Detective Schreffler. Sandusky admitted showering naked with Victim 6, admitted to hugging Victim 6 while in the shower and admitted that it was wrong. Detective Schreffler advised Sandusky not to shower with any child again and Sandusky said that he would not.

The Grand Jury was unable to subpoena B. K. because he is in the military and is stationed outside the United States.

Victim 7

About 1996 Sandusky took Victim 7, about twelve years old, to high school and Penn State football games. They showered together. The boy was very uncomfortable. There was touching on the thigh. According to the presentment, "Sandusky never touched any private parts of Victim 7."

Victim 8

Like Victim 2, Victim 8 was not identified by the authorities during the grand jury investigation. The presentment states:

> In the fall of 2000, a janitor named James "Jim" Calhoun ("Jim") observed Sandusky in the showers of the Lasch Building with a young boy pinned against the wall, performing oral sex on the boy. He immediately made known to other janitorial staff what he had just witnessed.
>
> At the time of the investigation Calhoun had dementia and could not testify. That same evening another employee saw the feet of two people in the shower. He later saw Sandusky exit the locker room holding hands with a young boy. Calhoun told his supervisor what he had seen. The boss "told him to whom he should report the incident, if he chose to report it."

Without specific attribution the presentment states, "In discussions held later that shift, the employees expressed concern that if they reported what Jim had seen, they might lose their jobs."

Calhoun, the witness, had developed dementia and could not testify at Sandusky's trial. Without a victim and without an eyewitness, it took some legerdemain to get a conviction for this alleged crime, but the prosecutors pulled it off.

14

4

The Investigation

The investigation leading to the presentment and indictment had been incredibly sloppy. The job of proving Sandusky was a serial child abuser fell to the aggressive prosecutors.

When the investigators learned of Victim 1 by a report from his school, they had a victim able to describe serious sexual abuse. Many experts believe Sandusky should have been arrested immediately. Instead, the investigation lasted three years. It was a strange investigation. They never caught this by-now-known pedophile with a victim. Where's the French Connection's Popeye Doyle? Didn't they stake this guy out some days after school, some Friday nights? Not only did they not catch Sandusky in the act, they didn't find one victim who was abused during the three-year investigation. Had Sandusky changed his ways? Not likely, from what we understand of pedophiles. Of course, after the investigation had dragged on for a while it would have been embarrassing to find child abuse that could have been prevented by an immediate arrest.

It appears that three of the victims had been found with the help of Victim 6, who was the boy involved in the 1998 incident that the prosecutors reopened. Two of these involved inappropriate touching but not actual sex acts.

15

To fill the gap, the prosecutors went back to 1998 and opened a case against Sandusky that had been closed. They received an anonymous tip that led them to McQueary. Investigative work may have turned up the janitor who had seen Sandusky in a Penn State shower with a boy. About one half of the presentment is devoted to these three cases—two without an identified victim and one that had been previously closed.

Of the six known victims at the time of the indictment there had been one reported incident of rape and that had been of slight penetration before the victim (Victim 4) resisted. After the charges against Sandusky became public, two men (Victims 9 and 10) came forward. Victim 9 claimed to have been raped multiple times by Sandusky. Victim 10 claimed he and Sandusky had oral sex.

5

The Sandusky Indictment

In November 2011, Sandusky was charged with over 40 child sex–related crimes, ranging from "involuntary deviate sexual intercourse" to "attempt to commit indecent assault." From the time of the indictment until the end of the trial, there could be no serious doubt that Sandusky was a serial pedophile.

Curley and Schultz were charged with perjury and failure to report.

After the indictments, the public concluded that football coach Joe Paterno, along with others at the Penn State University, had covered up a reported child rape in a Penn State shower room and had allowed a known pedophile to prey on young boys for years. The media and the public were outraged.

For Sandusky it came to an end on June 22, 2012, when he was convicted of 45 counts of sexually abusing 10 boys.

6

Tom "Remember The Children" Corbett

When they hand out prizes for sanctimonious hypocrite, Pennsylvania Governor Tom Corbett should get a blue ribbon. He was there when the investigation leading to Paterno's downfall began, and he was a mover in assuring that downfall.

In a later section, I will offer my cynical look at the American press. Perhaps all its members are not fools or knaves, but most of those who covered the Sandusky scandal are. ESPN had its share of mindless, uninformed commentators addressing the scandal, but it also had Don Van Natta, Jr., who, in ESPN's *Outside the Lines*, offered a well-researched, well-balanced account of Tom Corbett's role in the downfall of Penn State football. Much of the following is drawn from his account.

An overview of the shoddy investigation initiated under Corbett has been given. Van Natta adds details. As then–attorney general, after a victim claimed to have been subjected to oral sex by Sandusky, Corbett put one, or possibly two, investigators on the case. At the same time, the Republican attorney general had fourteen investigators on a case of alleged misuse of state funds for campaign purposes by a Democratic office holder. He turned his attention to corruption charges against both Republican and Democratic office holders. His investigation of Sandusky was so maddeningly slow the victim's mother complained to Federal officials.

Corbett later ran for governor. According to Van Natta, Corbett accepted almost $650,000 in campaign contributions from "current and past board members of Second Mile and their businesses." Corbett was investigating Sandusky and receiving big, big bucks from Sandusky associates. (Are you comfortable?) In November 2010 he was elected governor. In this position, he was, by law, a member of the Pennsylvania State University board of trustees.

Corbett, like most governors, was not a regular at board meetings. He missed the first four meeting during his time as governor. But Penn State was on his mind. During his first days in office he approved a $4 million grant to the Sandusky's charity and proposed to cut $184 million from the Penn State budget. (Who needs this guy on the Board?) University President Spanier attacked the governor for his "near total abandonment" of public higher education.

After missing the first four board meetings, reservations in State College were made for Corbett for the day before the November 2011 meeting. The reservations were made a week before the public learned of the charges against Sandusky.

A Penn State faculty member saw Corbett and his entourage at a State College restaurant. Corbett would later dispute the account that said "he was just effusive." It was during this time the board voted to oust Paterno. The ouster was done with a singular lack of taste; and it was the beginning of a chain of events with devastating consequences for the Penn State football program.

At a meeting Governor Corbett told the other Board members, "Remember the children." However, Corbett's saintly concern for the children had not been on display during his investigation of Sandusky.

7

Enter Louis Freeh

The Penn State Board of Trustees retained Freeh, Sporkin & Sullivan, LLP, the firm of retired FBI director Louis Freeh, to "perform an independent, full and complete investigation."

On July 12, 2012, the report of the investigation was released. The inflammatory language of the report's executive summary should have caused Penn State and the press to treat it with suspicion. They didn't.

The findings are not captioned; captions require a precision in language that was conspicuously absent. Here is the first "finding":

> The most saddening finding by the Special Investigative Counsel is the total and consistent disregard by the most senior leaders at Penn State for the safety and welfare of Sandusky's child victims. As the Grand Jury similarly noted in its presentment, there was no attempt to investigate, to identify Victim 2, or to protect that child or any others from similar conduct except as related to preventing its re-occurrence on University property.

This is wrong. Penn State officials took appropriate action to identify the boy—they notified Sandusky's charity. Officials there were in the best position to identify and assure the welfare of the child, who almost assuredly was under their care. They had a duty to do so.

The next "finding" asserts:

> Four of the most powerful people at the Pennsylvania State University—President Graham B. Spanier, Senior Vice President-Finance and Business Gary C. Schultz, Athletic Director Timothy M. Curley and Head Football Coach Joseph V. Paterno—failed to protect against a child sexual predator harming children for a decade. These men concealed Sandusky's activities from the Board of Trustees, the University community, and authorities. They exhibited a striking lack of empathy for Sandusky's victims by failing to inquire as to their safety and well-being especially by not attempting to determine the identity of the child who Sandusky assaulted in the Lasch Building in 2001. Further, they exposed this child to additional harm by alerting Sandusky, who was the only one who knew the child's identity, of what McQueary saw in the shower on the night of February 9, 2001.

Stripped of the highly charged language, we have this: "These men" failed to report "Sandusky's activities" to "the authorities." Are you kidding? All four men? What activities? What authorities? On the very core issue, Freeh offers this almost useless assessment. Why?

During the investigation, Penn State was receiving updates, and so too was the NCAA. During my career I undertook a number of investigations at the request of Congressional Committees. I was never asked for updates or partial reports.

Freeh now had two clients: The Penn State Board, which presumably wanted to know what happened, and the NCAA, which was itching to prove it was for apple pie and motherhood and bravely against child abuse. The objectives should be mutually exclusive. More likely, the Board of Trustees did not want an objective investigation any more than did the NCAA. The Board had removed Paterno from coaching with one home game remaining during the regular season. They had told the world that Paterno was complicit in the crime of child sexual abuse. After this destruction of a public figure's reputation, the Board needed proof of Paterno's guilt, a need not incongruent with the NCAA's desire to indict the entire football program.

Although the story involved football facilities, an ex-coach, and Paterno, there is no evidence the football program influenced the officials in handling the matter.

In an objective report, the language would be precise and measured. To serve Freeh's clients, the language had to be inflammatory and vague. It is clear what path he chose.

We now know that Sandusky was a child sexual predator. The sensational aspect of the language of the finding was that it asserted that in 1998, the officials *knew* he was a sexual predator.

In a loony claim, the report asserts, "[T]hey exposed this child to additional harm by alerting Sandusky who was the only one who knew the child's identity, of what McQueary saw in the shower." Sandusky already knew what McQueary saw in the shower. If they had tried to identify the boy on their own, how else could they have done it, other than by asking Sandusky?

The officials were criticized for allowing Sandusky "continued unrestricted and unsupervised access to the university's facilities." However, Sandusky had never been charged. Without charges, the university could have faced legal challenges to any effort to bar Sandusky from the campus or football events. The officials did want to bar him from bringing children into the facilities, but they seemed unable to enforce such a rule, then or earlier, when he retired. At that time, well before the McQueary incident, Sandusky wanted access to training and workout facilities. Paterno wrote on the proposal, "Is this for personal or 2nd mile kids. No to 2nd Mile. Liability problems." The investigators gave no explanation as to why this restriction by the all-powerful Paterno was not enforced.

A motive is offered—"in order to avoid the consequences of bad publicity." There is no support for this conclusion. "Sandusky's activities" were reported to the charitable organization.

The findings section ends with a list of factors, including "a lack of awareness of child abuse issues, the Clery Act and a football program that did not fully participate in, or opted out of some university programs, including Clery Act compliance." It cites "a culture of reverence for the football program that is ingrained at all levels of the campus community." It blames the men for allowing Sandusky to retire, "not as a suspected child predator, but as a valued member of the Penn State football legacy."

There is no effort to describe an unusual "reverence for the football program" or to distinguish Penn State culture from that of any big-time football university. There is no effort to link the football program to the actions of the Penn State officials in 2001. The report simply asserts what the NCAA wanted to hear.

Twice, the lack of compliance with the Clery Act is cited. This Federal Act requires the reporting of certain crimes, including sexual assaults, to local authorities, the keeping of a crime log, and, for statistical purposes, reporting of crimes on or near the campus of universities receiving federal funding.

Institutions are required to report Clery crimes that are "reported to campus security authorities or local police agencies" on an annual basis. Institutions are required to include any Clery crime in their collected statistics, even if there is no criminal charge filed or arrest made.

Under the law, Paterno and Curley and possibly McQueary are "campus security authorities." The question is, "Did McQueary see and report a crime?"

The most striking thing about the Freeh report is that the "findings" in the executive summary are not supported by a corresponding "findings" section in the body of the report. Each report chapter is headed by "Key Findings," but these are merely a collection of bullet points combining facts, innuendoes, and opinions. The Epilogue in this volume offers some examples of these "Key Findings."

Nowhere does Freeh marshal the evidence that McQueary had reported an act of child abuse. Can I stress that strongly enough? Nowhere does Freeh marshal the evidence that McQueary had reported an act of child abuse!

Nowhere does Freeh present evidence that the football culture informed the actions of the Penn State officials. In the executive summary, Freeh tells us the need to transform the culture is "illustrated throughout this report." What? On this critical matter, couldn't you have been a tad bit more specific, Louis?

8

The 1998 Incident

The claim in the executive summary of the Freeh report that Sandusky was a "suspected child predator" when he retired is as wrong as it is inflammatory.

In 1998, the mother of a young boy reported a possible sexual assault on her son on the Penn State campus. Thirteen years later, prosecutors would revisit this case. The boy would become Victim 6 in the Grand Jury presentment. Freeh would use it to shamelessly accuse Penn State officials of wrongdoing, when there had been no wrongdoing on their part.

The mother became concerned when she learned her son had showered with Sandusky. She consulted a psychologist and called the police, and the boy reported to the police he showered with Sandusky. This psychologist was the only diligent professional involved. She met the boy and reported the incident to the Pennsylvania child abuse line. Sandusky admitted he had showered with boys in the past. The psychologist and her colleagues thought "the incidents meet all of our definitions, based on experience and education, of a likely pedophile's pattern." There is no evidence that this professional opinion ever reached Penn State officials. But the police and prosecutor's office had access to it.

The Department of Public Welfare sought an opinion from their counselor. He found no evidence of sexual abuse and no pattern suggesting pedophilia. No charges against Sandusky were filed.

Penn State officials followed this matter, but Freeh concluded that the officials made no attempt to influence the investigation. (The football culture must have been asleep.) Spanier did not formally bring this matter to the attention of the board of trustees. There was nothing else remotely improper about the Penn State actions—and even this may not have been improper.[2] Freeh charges the officials with not treating a man as a "suspected child abuser" after he had been cleared of all charges.

There was some dispute about how closely the front office had followed the investigation. As Sandusky was still a coach, we can suspect there was considerable interest. My initial reaction on learning of this event was that it didn't much matter. The more the officials knew of it, the more clearly they knew that authorities had found no crime when a man showered with a boy.

Freeh put the most nefarious twist imaginable on this episode. He used it to conclude that the Penn State officials repeatedly concealed evidence of a pedophile. This is sheer nonsense, but it worked. The NCAA vacated all Penn State victories from the year of this incident.

In August 2012, Eileen Morgan presented a critical analysis of the Freeh report on the Jerry Sandusky scandal. She examines key elements of the Freeh report, including its treatment of this 1998 incident. In her analysis she demonstrates how Freeh manipulated and misinterpreted e-mails to charge Paterno and Spanier with following the matter more closely than they apparently did. She quotes the Freeh report on the Penn State officials and the 1998 investigation:

> Despite their knowledge of the criminal investigation of Sandusky, Spanier, Schultz, Paterno and Curley took no action to limit Sandusky's access to Penn State facilities or took any measures to protect children on their campus.

---

[2] From the available information, we do not know how much the Penn State officials knew and how much they shared about this investigation. Ray Blehar, who had served in national intelligence, has written that the Pennsylvania law on child abuse investigations would have made it illegal for Spanier or Schultz to have shared information on an ongoing investigation.

Morgan observes:

Makes absolutely no sense. Why would the PSU officials limit Sandusky's access to PSU facilities? He was a coach and he was found innocent of any wrongdoing by the law enforcement and the DA. Why would Penn State officials need to protect children on their campus? The authorities determined that the children were not being abused, so why would the children need protection from Sandusky. Even though the DA dropped the charges against Sandusky in 1998, Freeh is writing this report as if Jerry Sandusky was tried and convicted of being a child molester in 1998 and that the PSU officials knew this and did nothing about it. However, the antithesis is true, Sandusky was not charged with any crime and was free to carry on, working at Second Mile where he was around a multitude of boys day in and day out. So the authorities obviously were not concerned that the children of Second Mile were in any danger.

Here Morgan exposes the particular lunacy of Freeh, the NCAA, and the press in criticizing Penn State for the 1998 incident. No matter what Penn State had done that year, Sandusky would have been free to use his position at The Second Mile to find and exploit new victims. Many of his crimes were not committed on University grounds and while his University connection was useful in furthering his crimes, it was hardly essential.

With regard to the investigators' conclusion that there had been no crime, Freeh reported:

Had the officers been better trained in the investigations of child sexual abuse they would have interrogated Sandusky directly after his confrontation with the boy's mother. A timely interview with Sandusky may have elicited candid responses such as the identification of other victims.

Morgan comments:

Wait a minute. Freeh has accused a football coach, an athletic director, a VP of Finance and Business and a school President (who are not trained in child sexual abuse) for not doing enough to take Sandusky to the proper authorities in 2001 to get him off the street, away from young boys, but gives a free pass to the 1998 actual law enforcement team who were paid and trained to protect society?

Maybe the 2001 report had more specific details than the 1998 allegations, but the best evidence indicates it did not. Morgan makes a nice point in ridiculing Freeh's excuse for the authorities.

Freeh goes out of his way to show that Paterno was following this matter closely. He quotes two e-mails. In one Curley writes to Schultz, "I have touched base with the coach, keep us posted." In the other Curley writes, "Anything new in this Department? Coach is anxious to know." Freeh concludes that "coach" in both e-mails refers to Paterno. Morgan points out that the e-mail about "touching base" has in the subject line "Paterno," and the e-mail about "anxious to know" has in the subject line "Sandusky."

With far more logic than Freeh, Morgan concludes that the "touching base" coach was likely Paterno, and the "anxious to know" coach was defensive coordinator Sandusky. But Freeh is single-minded in his efforts to indict Paterno.

In any event, I remain baffled as to why knowledge of this incident, when it was found by authorities that a man showering with a boy was not a crime, reflects adversely on the Penn State officials. I am still searching for the Penn State misconduct found by Freeh, and later the NCAA, concerning this incident.

9

The Janitor Incident

One can only assume (as there is no way to be sure) that one incident, described and footnoted, represents the body of evidence showing that reform of the football culture is needed. The report describes an incident in 2000, where a janitor allegedly saw Sandusky performing oral sex on a boy in a Penn State shower. The janitor told another janitor. They told their supervisor. This unknown victim became Victim 8 in the grand jury presentment. The attack was not reported beyond that. The first janitor has dementia. The second janitor told the Freeh investigators that Paterno would have had them fired if they had reported the matter. The investigators take this lame excuse for not performing a civic duty at face value. Did the janitors know of a case of recrimination against an employee? How did they think Paterno would have gotten involved? We aren't told. This is apparently the only basis the investigators have to denounce the "culture," and it was accepted without question.

Since the janitor wasn't asked to explain his fear, the investigators take a stab at it. A footnote makes a vague reference to an incident involving the athletic department and football players in 2007, much later than the incident involving Victim 8. This brief citation in a footnote of a 2007 incident to explain the janitors' fears in 2000 seems to be the best Freeh can do.

10

The Indictment Revisited

When prosecutors brought the Sandusky affair to public attention, with a number of known victims, why did they include unknown Victim 2? Maybe because, as noted, they had very little to show for their three-year investigation. Furthermore, did they use the Penn State connection to divert attention from a more serious failing of prosecutors thirteen years early? If that was their intention, it worked. All media outrage has been directed at Penn State, and none at the law enforcement officials who had ignored evidence against Sandusky.

Maybe the prosecutors wanted to downplay the fact that it had taken three years of investigation to bring the 2011 charges against Sandusky. This reportedly understaffed investigation had been started by Tom Corbett, who at the time was Pennsylvania's attorney general, and at the time of the indictments, was the Commonwealth's governor.

Perhaps the Commonwealth wanted to protect the Second Mile charity. Officials of this charity had donated generously to support the Corbett's political career. As governor, Corbett had approved a multimillion-dollar grant to the charity while Sandusky was under investigation. By throwing the spotlight on Penn State, the prosecutors diverted attention from the fact that this organization had harbored a pedophile for years.

11

The McQueary Account
And Paterno, Curley,
Schultz, And Spanier

While outside the shower room, McQueary called his father. He then went home and spoke to his father, and his father's friend and boss, a medical doctor. These men must have heard the most emotional account prior to McQueary's legal testimony, because they heard it soon after the event. They did not advise going to the police. The doctor was not part of "the Penn State football culture." According to the Freeh report, "John McQueary advised his son to report the matter to Paterno, and neither John McQueary nor his boss advised him to immediately call the police." The report's use of the word "immediately" here is telling. Freeh has to deal with the fact that no one thought McQueary's account deserved police notification, but he is not willing to concede that obvious point. Thus we have Freeh's inclusion of the word "immediately."

Alice would be right at home in this wonderland, because it gets curiouser and curiouser. There is no evidence in the Freeh report that his team interviewed McQueary's father or the family friend.

The report asserts that the team conducted over 430 interviews, but it did not interview some individuals because it was requested not to do so by the Pennsylvania attorney general. Perhaps these two critical witnesses were among the banned. At the Sandusky trial, the doctor testified under oath that he asked McQueary multiple times what he had seen, and McQueary said nothing of having seen anything sexual. He said McQueary spoke of hearing "sexual sounds" before entering the shower room, but their nature, during the couple of seconds of McQueary's exposure to the incident, is unexplained. Whatever McQueary told the doctor, it didn't prompt a recommendation to notify the police.

Whoever those 430 interviewees were, they did not include any of the six men with firsthand knowledge of what McQueary said he saw—not McQueary; not his father or his father's friend; and not Paterno, Curley, or Schultz.

The Freeh team found brief e-mails between Spanier, Schultz, and Curley related to their actions after receiving McQueary's account. One fact is clear: the Penn State officials came close to reporting the matter to the Department of Public Welfare. Why Public Welfare and not the police?

The question of whether the failure to report to the Department of Welfare was a crime is still before the courts. Soon after McQueary reported what he saw, the university's outside counsel billed Penn State for 2.9 hours of time for a phone conversation with Schultz. The subject was "reporting of suspected child abuse." Later, in a handwritten note, the writer (apparently Schultz) said:

> "3) Tell chair" of Board of Second Mile 2) Report to Dept of Welfare. (1 Tell JS to avoid bringing children alone into Lasch Bldg." 'Who's the chair??

In an e-mail dated February 27, 2001, Curley told Schultz and Spanier:

> After giving it more thought and talking it over with Joe yesterday, I am uncomfortable with what we agreed were the next steps. I am having trouble with going to everyone, but the person involved. I think I would be more comfortable meeting with the person and tell him about

the information we received. I would plan to tell him we are aware of the first situation. I would indicate we feel there is a problem and we want to assist the individual to get professional help. Also, we feel a responsibility at some point soon to inform his organization and [sic] maybe the other one about the situation. If he is cooperative we would work with him to handle informing the organization. If not we have no choice and will inform the two groups. Additionally, I will let him know that his guests are not permitted to use our facilities. I need some help on this one. What do you think about this approach?

On February 27, 2001, Spanier e-mailed Curley and Schultz:

Tim;

This approach is acceptable to me. It requires you to go a step further and means that your conversation will be all the more difficult, but I admire your willingness to do that and I am supportive. The only downside to us is if the message isn't "heard" and acted upon, and we then become vulnerable for not having reported it. But that can be assessed down the road. The approach you outline is humane and a responsible way to proceed.

On February 28, 2001, Schultz e-mailed Curley and Spanier:

Tim and Graham, this is a more humane and upfront way to handle this. I can support this approach, with the understanding that we will inform his organization, with or without his cooperation (I think that's what Tim proposed.)We can play it by ear to decide about the other organization.

"Covering up" was not an option. McQueary had not been sworn to secrecy. When asked under oath if the officials had told him not to talk to anybody about it, McQueary responded, "No. No. They never said don't talk to anybody". McQueary's father knew; and a friend, a medical doctor, not connected to Penn State, also knew. They reported it to Sandusky's charitable organization, so others knew as well. And the boy knew. Who knew when this boy might speak up? A "cover-up" was not available. They took no action to achieve one.

The website *The Framing of Joe Paterno* has a brilliant animated satire where Paterno tells Curley they have to cover it up, and Curley asks, "Why tell me about it?" Paterno then points out that "Only five people and the child" know about it.

These men did not see reporting the incident as harming the reputation of Penn State. If Sandusky continued to bring boys onto campus, it could prove embarrassing if they *did not* now report. This turns the Freeh conclusion on motive on its head. Nowhere is there a hint of a pervasive football culture. Why not report? When Curley told Spanier that he planned to approach Sandusky, Spanier responded, "[Y]our conversation will be all the more difficult, but I admire your willingness to do that." This deference to Sandusky does not spring from the football culture. Greater deference was shown to Sandusky, perhaps the second best-known figure in Happy Valley, by law enforcement officials in 1998.

The most likely motive for not going to the Department of Welfare is that they did not want to create a public record against this respected individual on the basis of a suspicion. They mistakenly believed reporting to the charity would be sufficient to initiate a proper investigation. If they had reported to the Department of Welfare, as they were on the verge of doing, the Department may have called on the counselor who "saw no evil" three years earlier, and he may have seen no evil again. Nevertheless it would have been prudent for Curley or Schultz to have brought a suspicious matter involving a child to the appropriate professionals, even if they had no legal responsibility to do so.

Two questions left unanswered are (1) what was said in the phone conversation between the attorney and Schultz, and (2) what are the details of the conversation between Paterno and Curley mentioned in the e-mail? Whatever transpired during these conversations, the details could hardly define or indict an entire football program.

Attorneys for Spanier issued a critique of the Freeh report. In the critique they reported that the attorney consulted by Schultz "recently informed Dr. Spanier that although he does not recall the specific consultation in 2001, he (Courtney) reported that he must have concluded that the 2001 episode was not reportable, since if it had been reportable, he would have insisted that it be reported and would have documented that advice in his file." Are we to infer from this that Schultz never told Spanier of his discussion with Courtney?

To satisfy the NCAA, Freeh had to include Paterno in all failings. Yet it was Paterno who caused the matter to be brought to the highest levels of Penn State. Schultz and Curley were the key players. Schultz alone had spoken to both McQueary and to the outside counsel on "reporting of suspected child abuse." Spanier, the president of the university, had been brought into the matter. He was the only one of the four to have been interviewed. It seems the investigators never asked Spanier if Schultz had shared the advice he had received from the attorney on reporting suspected child abuse. If these facts were available, one could better determine why the matter was resolved the way it was. The Freeh investigators seemed to be the gang that couldn't shoot straight.

12

The McQueary Account Examined Or Not Examined By Freeh

The prosecutors charged Sandusky with rape of Victim 2, even though McQueary never claimed to have seen a rape. He provided the Grand Jury and, later the Sandusky trial jury, with a lurid account of what he saw, which did not include rape. Evidence is that his prior accounts were more benign.

At the Sandusky trial, when McQueary's father testified about his son's account, he couldn't remember testifying at the preliminary hearing. Michael McCann of the Vermont Institute of Sports Law has criticized Sandusky's defense attorneys for not questioning the inconsistency of the father's testimony with prior statements. McCann also believed a case could have been made that the testimony had been "enhanced" by "prosecutor coaching." Even though McQueary never said he saw a rape, it seems certain his testimony was more lurid than anything he told the Penn State officials. Why? It is very likely his testimony was also "enhanced." McQueary was now in front of the prosecutors. He was scared. What he had seen had never been reported to the authorities.

It's pretty clear McQueary is not the sharpest guy to ever open a playbook. Imagine the prosecutor giving this speech:

> *Fella, you really screwed up. If you had done right back in 2001, this sexual predator would have been off the street. You owe it to everybody to set it straight. We got the bastard cold. But we only got one other rape victim, and we have no eyewitness for that one. We got plenty of other assaults, but we don't want to go before a damn jury with just one rape and no eyewitness. This guy is a serial rapist. You sure as hell saw a rape. You're an eye-witness, and you better admit it.*

We don't know what transpired between the prosecutors and McQueary, but it was likely something like that. Now, McQueary doesn't want to say he saw a rape for two reasons: (1) he didn't, and (2) it would make him look even worse. He goes as far as he can in describing a physical attack short of insertion. The prosecutors filled in that gap. In any event, what McQueary ended up telling authorities certainly had little resemblance to what he told the Penn State officials.

McCann thought that with a stronger defense Sandusky's attorneys "may have convinced jurors that they cannot believe, beyond a reasonable doubt, in the charges related to victim 2." Look how close we came to no case against Penn State! A legal expert saw the possibility of "reasonable doubt," which is almost tantamount to seeing actual "reasonable doubt." Imagine if Curley and Schultz had not been facing their own criminal charges. They would have been available for the defense to rebut McQueary's account. That might have moved the case from *possible* reasonable doubt to *more than* reasonable doubt.

During the Sandusky trial, with McQueary on the stand, the judge called the attorneys up for a sidebar and said to the prosecutor, "I don't know why you're not getting objections to these grossly misleading questions." The judge asked for caution. The prosecutor said he was just trying to get through it. We don't know why the defense did not object to "grossly misleading questions," but the prosecutor continued unchallenged, asking such questions as "Did you tell him what you had seen?" rather than "What did you tell him?"

Reading the testimony, it is painful to watch McQueary give the prosecutors the vivid account they want while admitting his reports to others were far less specific. At one stage, he says what he saw was "extremely sexual"; at another point he says he called his father because he just saw "something ridiculous".

"Ridiculous" is a man showering with a boy at night. It is not sexual abuse. In describing his account to Paterno, McQueary uses the phase "on the surface" and says he was sure Paterno knew the event was sexual. Not once does he say he *told* Paterno it was sexual.

The prosecutors' case against Sandusky for Victim 2 hung by a thread. It was a thread that was stretched but did not break. In the end, the jury found Sandusky not guilty of rape but guilty of lesser crimes involving Victim 2. And it was on the thread of these crimes that the NCAA hung Joe Paterno.

By avoiding any effort to determine what McQueary told the Penn State officials, Freeh left in place the mistaken belief that McQueary reported a rape. Where McCann, an objective observer, saw the possibility that there was reasonable doubt that McQueary saw a crime, Freeh had no doubt at all. Freeh's sensational conclusions all revolved around the assertion that the Penn State officials knew Sandusky was a pedophile. He never showed us how he reached this conclusion. How did Freeh reconcile Paterno's statement that he was told of McQueary seeing something of a sexual nature with the medical doctor's statements that McQueary specifically denied seeing something sexual? Paterno's vague recollections had not been tested by cross-examination. Freeh didn't even try.

Throughout this self-proclaimed independent investigation, the Freeh team operated as an extension of the prosecutors. In one finding, the investigators state, "As the Grand Jury similarly noted in its presentment...." Their deference to the attorney general and the prosecutors invalidates the entire investigation.

At the heart of the matter for the Penn State officials was not what McQueary saw, but what he reported. The two Penn State officials facing charges of perjury understandably would not talk to the investigators. Paterno was in the last days of his life when the investigation began. It's not clear the investigators ever intended to interview him. He passed away before the investigation ended, and they did not speak to him. But there was no reason not to have tried to interview McQueary, his father, and his father's friend, except to honor a request made by the Attorney General. Of the six men with firsthand knowledge of what McQueary initially reported, the investigators interviewed none. None! Having accepted an extreme limitation on their investigation, they should have found some way to examine the matter. They could have applied their forensic skills to comparing and analyzing the various accounts of what McQueary reported. They could have gone into the shower room and reenacted the incident, based on McQueary's accounts. None of this was done. During the Sandusky trial, the defense, with photographs of the shower room, tried to reconstruct McQueary's account. It was confusing, and when reading the testimony without the benefit of the photos, it is impossible to follow the explanation. But this was an important area ignored by Freeh.

There was another avenue for Freeh to explore the events in the shower that night. There are accounts that soon after Sandusky's arrest the prosecutors and the defense leaned the identity of Victim 2. According to these accounts the prosecutors couldn't call him as a witness because his initial report to investigators was that on the night he was seen in the shower by McQueary, there had been no abuse. Let's repeat that. There are reports that Victim 2 has claimed McQueary could not have seen him abused. But, according to the accounts, the defense did not call him because he claimed to have been abused by Sandusky on other occasions. Is the man claiming to be Victim 2 really Victim 2? Did he tell investigators he was not abused when seen by McQueary? Did the Freeh team know of the existence of this guy? If not, why not? If they did, why didn't they address it in their report? If the story is true the prosecutors had a duty to drop the charges involving the McQueary incident and add charges supported by the witness's accounts.

Ten years after the McQueary report, Paterno testified before the grand jury that he was told there was "fondling, whatever you might call it, I'm not sure what the term might be—a young boy." After another question, he repeats, "Well, I don't know what you would call it. Obviously he was doing something with the youngster. It was a sexual nature. I'm not sure exactly what it was."

Here is the case against Paterno. And it's in his own words. But he couldn't recall any of the words McQueary had used, saying "I don't know what you would call it." The question is, what did *McQueary* call it? Paterno didn't remember. In McQueary's various accounts, he never described his observations as having lasted long enough for him to have seen "fondling." In his testimony at the Sandusky trial, McQueary never claimed to have used the words "sex" or "sexual" in his account to Paterno.

At 8:40 on the morning of Paterno's Grand Jury testimony, he was interviewed by the police. He was accompanied by an attorney and his son, Scott, who is also an attorney. Also present were two attorneys from the Attorney General's office. Paterno said that McQueary had told him he saw something "inappropriate" in the shower room, involving Sandusky and a young boy. Paterno said McQueary didn't give him any "specific details" but that McQueary was upset.

We don't know where Paterno, his attorney, or his son were during the next couple of hours before he took the stand in front of the grand jury. We also don't know where the two government attorneys were. After the police interviewed Paterno, they interviewed Schultz and Curley. The government attorneys who attended the Paterno interview did not attend those two interviews. What did they have to do that was more important? Could they have spent time with Paterno, telling him McQueary's recall was that he had told Paterno of fondling, and that there was something sexual in the scene? That's imaginative speculation. But what else explains the eighty-four-year-old Paterno's memory of an event ten years earlier changing from "inappropriate" to "sexual nature"; from no "specific details" to "fondling, I don't know what you would call it"? That change took place in the span of two hours. What happened?

Others have pointed out that with testimony this confused and inconsistent it would have been very helpful to have actually heard the witness. Were his statements made with authority? Doubtful. Were there inflections suggesting he was more asking than telling? Possible.

One of the last versions of what Paterno knew came on October 1, 2012, when Commonwealth prosecutors responded to a motion to have the trials of Schultz and Curley severed. In arguing against the motion the Commonwealth makes this statement, "According to testimony presented at the preliminary hearing Michael McQueary, then a graduate assistant football coach, reported to Paterno that he had witnessed Sandusky in a shower with a boy." That probably comes closer to the truth than any other version we have heard. In a footnote the prosecutors add "Precisely what McQueary saw and reported and what Paterno reported is a matter that the parties dispute. For present purposes, it is sufficient to say that McQueary testified that he believed that Paterno and the defendants understood that Sandusky's conduct was sexual in nature."

Even the aggressive prosecutors now refuse to claim that McQueary told Paterno he had seen a sexual act. But the world has been led to believe otherwise.

13

The Football
Program Condemed

On November 9, 2011, with one remaining home game, Joe Paterno was removed from coaching by the Board of Trustees. Board Vice Chairman John Surma announced, "The University is much larger than its football program." With nothing other than the Grand Jury Presentment, which offered unproven charges, the Board of Trustees had told the world that Joe Paterno, along with his entire program, were guilty of complicity in a child abuse scandal. Paterno had asked to speak to the Board, but that courtesy wasn't extended.

The Freeh report and the NCAA actions followed, as night follows day. And a dark night it was.

In January 2012, Paterno gave an interview to *Washington Post* columnist Sally Jenkins. In the interview, Paterno told Jenkins, "If Sandusky is guilty, I'm sick about it." Despite what he told the Grand Jury, Paterno apparently was not certain what he had heard. Jenkins tried to give a balanced account, but she couldn't avoid the scandal's emotional trap. She reported that McQueary had told Paterno of a "shocking scene." There is no evidence for that. Immediately after the Freeh report became public Jenkins had written, "Joe Paterno was a liar. There's no doubt about that now." Actually there was doubt. Jenkins quoted the "Coach is anxious to know" email, and there is doubt that "coach" in this case was Paterno.

For the interview, Jenkins was in Paterno's home. Paterno told Jenkins, "I was afraid to jeopardize what the University policy was. So I backed away and turned it over to some people I thought would have a little more expertise than I did. It didn't work out that way."

This is typical Paterno—logical, disciplined. But the press and the public seem to have wanted him to change character and become something he was not.

Freeh appeared determined to indict Paterno. The prosecutors had charged Schultz and Curley with failure to report, but not Paterno. Freeh, in his "failure to report" finding, threw in Paterno and Spanier. Did Freeh charge only Spanier, or maybe Spanier and Schultz, with a failure to inform the Board of Trustees? No, he includes Paterno in that charge. Why Paterno?

Freeh's biggest challenge was when he addressed the available evidence of the deliberations on how the McQueary report was to be handled. The Freeh report cites a couple of handwritten notes. Paterno didn't write them, and he's not mentioned in them. The report cites a few e-mails. Paterno doesn't send or receive e-mail. But wait. Paterno is mentioned in one—just one. Guess what? The one e-mail with Paterno's name in it is leaked to the press. Freeh then misquotes and mischaracterizes it.

In a chapter summary, Freeh describes the e-mail: "[H]e (Curley) has changed his mind about the plan 'after giving it more thought and talking it over with Joe (Paterno) yesterday,' Curley now proposes to tell Sandusky 'we feel there is a problem' and offer him professional help."

Freeh ends the quote after "Joe yesterday," inserts his own words, and then goes back to the quote with "we feel." Presented in this fashion, it appears the "we" is Paterno and Curley. This is a deliberate distortion. In context, the "we" refers to Curley, Schultz, and Spanier.

Freeh asserts that after the discussion with Paterno, Curley "has changed his mind about the plan," leaving the impression that, because of Paterno, a plan is now in place that does not include reporting to authorities. This is inaccurate. In this e-mail, after the reference to Joe, Curley still leaves the door open to reporting to "the other organization." The "other organization" is clearly the Department of Public Welfare. After this one mention of Paterno, the plan is still not finalized. The day after this e-mail, Schultz sends an e-mail to Curley and Spanier, writing, "We can play it by ear to decide about the other organization." Whatever influence Paterno had on these deliberations (it appears it was minimal or nonexistent), he had not closed the door to a report to the authorities. It may not have been Freeh who leaked the e-mail, but he's my prime suspect. Freeh clearly tried to make Paterno the crucial mover of the eventual plan that did not include reporting to the authorities. This is not objectivity. This is dishonesty—and, given the stakes, dishonesty of a very high order.

When the e-mail suggesting that Paterno caused Curley to abandon the plan to notify the Department of Public Welfare was leaked, it was not the first time Freeh was connected to a leak that had incited an irresponsible press.

In July 1996, Richard Jewell, one of many security guards for the Olympic games in Atlanta, Georgia, found what appeared to be a pipe bomb. He notified the Georgia authorities and, with others, began clearing the area. The bomb exploded, killing one and injuring many. Jewell became a hero. But soon the press was reporting that the FBI was looking at him as a suspect. News articles of almost unbelievable irresponsibility followed, painting the one-time hero as a failed, sad-looking loser and almost certain terrorist. In the end, it was found he was a hero. The real terrorist was caught. Jewell won damages from news organizations, and FBI chief Freeh went before a Senate committee to address how the leak from the FBI had occurred. After all, the FBI had a strict policy against leaks. With all the powers of the FBI, Freeh was never able to identify the leaker.

The Freeh report quoted unnamed sources expressing the view that Curley was Paterno's errand boy. True or not, it was irrelevant. Neither Paterno nor Curley was in a position to call the final shots.

Freeh never missed a chance to bash Paterno. In his press conference—yes, the independent investigator chose to go before the press—Freeh made a series of sensational, unsubstantiated charges, some aimed directly at Paterno. The first page of the critique of the Freeh report by attorneys for Spanier says the following:

> Before having seen the Report, the Board of Trustees agreed to waive attorney-client privilege and allow FSS Senior Managing Partner Louis J. Freeh, in the style of a criminal prosecutor, to hold a national press conference announcing the findings. None of the individuals condemned by the Report was given an opportunity to review the Report, much less to offer a rebuttal, before it was published to the nation.

Freeh never explored why the notification to The Second Mile was not sufficient to end Sandusky's crimes. The Freeh investigators handled The Second Mile with kid gloves. Curley met with the executive director of The Second Mile. The executive director refused to grant an interview to the Freeh investigators. This didn't seem to trouble the investigators. Counsel for The Second Mile told the investigators that Curley had told the executive director that after talking with Sandusky, he had concluded "nothing inappropriate occurred." It's hard to imagine Curley going over there to report nothing. However, we haven't heard directly from either party.

The unspoken cynicism in this whole matter revolves around why the press, Freeh, and the NCAA found the alert by Penn State officials to The Second Mile to have been an inadequate response. Apparently, in their heart of hearts, they believed the Penn State officials should have known The Second Mile officials would protect their great meal ticket, even if he was a pedophile. No one had the right to silently transfer their utter cynicism to the men at Penn State. They should tell us why notification to the organization that was almost certainly responsible for the young boy didn't result in an internal investigation.

Coach Paterno made sure the incident was reported to Schultz. An outside attorney and the university's President were brought in. Paterno participated little in the subsequent discussions. Soon after Sandusky's indictment, Paterno was removed from coaching. He is perhaps the first American in history to have been fired for *not* blowing the whistle. And in this case it seems there was no apparent need to blow a whistle. The Freeh report devotes considerable attention to university policies, but it doesn't tell us if Paterno would have been in compliance with Penn State policy if he had taken the matter further.

It was the University President who approved the final course of action, including a report to Sandusky's charitable organization but no report to the Department of Welfare. It included a weak effort to keep Sandusky out of the Penn State showers. Nothing suggests this decision was made in deference to the football program.

The eyes of the nation were on Paterno. It was vital for Freeh to describe Paterno's failings. He didn't. Yet, the NCAA punished the football program and, in a particularly weird act, vacated all Paterno's football victories from 1998.

In the words of William Wirt during the famous Aaron Burr treason trial, we can ask, "Is this reason? Is this law? Is it humanity?"

What did Freeh, the Board of Trustees, the NCAA, and the media want Paterno to do? Could he not safely assume that the university's top administrative official, the university's president, and The Second Mile charity would properly handle the matter?

Paterno didn't let the matter drop. In testimony at the Curley/Schultz Preliminary Hearing in December, 2011, McQueary testified that twice after the incident Paterno had asked him if he was "OK' with it. So we know that twice Paterno invited the only witness to say if more should be done, and twice the witness declined to do so. McQueary also testified that he told Curley he was "OK" with the actions taken.

Was Paterno to go to the police with a secondhand account, when the only witness had no inclination to do so? McQueary, his father, the family friend, Curley, Shultz, Spanier, and the executive director at the charity all passed on the opportunity to bring the matter to the authorities.

Every university president who voted to impose the sanctions should offer to answer the following questions:

1. You have stripped Joe Paterno of his victories since 1998. *What do you believe Paterno should have done differently that year?*

2. You have punished the entire football program.

    a. *What do you believe Paterno should have done differently in 2001?*

    b. *If a similar situation had arisen at your university, and the coach had taken the matter to outside authorities after the university president had approved a course of actions, would that coach have violated any university policy?*

    c. *On what basis do you extend your disapproval of Paterno's actions or lack of actions to the football program?*

No one has found a way to get the NCAA into court on this matter. They would probably assert that Penn State had invited the sanctions. Nevertheless, wouldn't justice be served if each president who voted for the sanctions were put on the stand or deposed and asked these questions? Absent that, is there an enterprising reporter who will solicit answers to these questions?

Speaking for the NCAA on the sanctions, Mark Emmert said:

> One of the grave dangers stemming from our love of sports is that the sports themselves become too big to fail, indeed, too big to even challenge. The results can be the erosion of academic values that are replaced by the value of hero worship and winning at all costs.

No one asked him how the football program was being protected from failure. No one asked him how "hero worship" played a role in what transpired. And the NCAA certainly didn't find any erosion of academic values at Penn State. If Penn State ever committed a recruiting violation, it was not reported by Freeh. If Penn

State athletes ever unfairly received favorable academic treatment, it remained unreported by Freeh.

During the memorial following his death, Paterno was praised by a university dean for supporting the school's liberal arts program. Paterno and his wife, Sue, gave generously to the university library that bears their name. I once read that Paterno believed that if a disaster destroyed all the buildings on a university campus except the library, it would still be a university. The graduation rate of his football players is among the highest in Division 1 football. This had been one of the most unstained college football programs of our lifetime.

On September 12, 2012, the *Centre Daily Times* ran a story with the headline REPORT CASTS DOUBT ON CLAIMS OF SPORTS-CENTRIC CULTURE. The article references a study done in 2007 that had found no improper sports culture at Penn State. According to the article, Robert Secor, Vice Provost Emeritus, said he was at Penn State for 35 years and "when a student-athlete in his class was having a difficult time, he would sometimes get a call from a coach asking what could be done to help the student do well in the class such as tutoring. The pressure was on the student not him."

Professor Victor Brunsden is quoted: "If there is a football culture, what are the signs of it, and where? What do you mean by that?" Those are questions Freeh never answered. Brunsden also asked, "Does it mean we're very proud of our football team? OK. Guilty. You got me. Are we willing to give good grades to our players, just simply because of the team? Not that I'm aware of."

Why didn't one of the over 430 interviews conducted by the Freeh investigators turn up this report? How could it be ignored in an evaluation of the football culture at Penn State? .

The unjustified sanctions imposed by the NCAA on July 23, 2012, had been accompanied by a consent decree signed by Penn State. This signing apparently bars the university from challenging the sanctions. Penn State claims they had a choice of signing the decree or having the NCAA shut down the football program entirely for a number of years. It has been reported by ESPN's Dan

Van Natta, Jr. that many of the university presidents with NCAA votes wanted the "death penalty."

The NCAA sanctions banned Penn State from bowl games for four years and reduced the number of its football scholarships. The NCAA fined Penn State $60 million, with the money to go to a program for victims of child abuse. Appropriately, given the other penalties, football players were allowed to transfer to other schools and play football without the customary waiting period.

An NCAA spokesman had said collegiate sports programs cannot be allowed to be too big to fail or to be challenged. He had cited an erosion of academic values. When asked how they reached their conclusions without an investigation, they cited the Freeh report. There is nothing in the Freeh report to justify condemning the football program. The New American Foundation gave an academic rating to the twenty-five teams that ranked highest in the football Bowl Championship series for 2011. Penn State came out on top, with a numerical grade of 107. For comparison, Stanford had a grade of 100; and Michigan, 31. I don't know how valid this effort is in measuring the academic side of big-time football, but how does the NCAA justify condemning the Penn State football program?

Drastic NCAA actions, taken without an investigation, were justified by reference to a dishonest report. Officials at Penn State consented to the sanctions, saying that without consent, the penalties would have been much harsher. John Adams once said the law is "deaf, deaf as an adder, to the clamors of the populace." The NCAA, unrestrained by due process restrictions, was free to cower before the clamors of the populace—and its ruling members did cower. The presidents of 18 American universities personally contributed to this injustice.

The choice of four years for a bowl ban was cruel and unusual. The young men who stay with the program will have few chances to experience the joy of a bowl game.

There are some heroes. Most of the young men who play for, or have committed to play for Penn State, have indicated they are staying with the program. I am not questioning the players who make the decision to transfer; I am suggesting there is something honorable in those who chose to stay with their university. There is certainly nothing honorable to be found in the NCAA.

There was a human interest story connected with one transfer. Kicker-punter Anthony Fera transferred to Texas. Some news accounts simply mentioned the transfer. Some noted the special circumstance that illness in his family now made it more difficult for his mother and father to travel from Texas to the east to see his games. None that I found mentioned this part of his statement: "I made a promise to coach Paterno and my family the day I arrived on campus to obtain a degree from Penn State University, which with the cooperation of the folks at Texas, I plan to fulfill over the next year. I will always proudly say that I am a Penn State alum."

This is a nice little story. The young man's respect for Paterno and Paterno's respect for education are on display. This is not a story line the media wished to acknowledge.

14

A Free Press
In Action

On July 29, 2012, the television program *Face the Nation* had a segment titled "The Penn State Football Scandal." Bob Schieffer interviewed Penn State President Rodney Erickson and hosted a panel discussion. The panel participants displayed a strong dislike for big-time football or Penn State football. Schieffer was clearly befuddled by it all. He referred to a "cover up" and told Erickson he did not understand why the men "did not try to tell someone about it." Erickson shared his puzzlement. Erickson didn't bother to point out that the men not only tried to "tell someone," they *did* tell someone. A responsible response from a Penn State representative would have been something like this: "That's simply not true, Bob. They *did* report it to Sandusky's charitable organization."

When Schieffer asked Erickson if football at Penn State had gotten too big, Erickson responded that the football program had perhaps become too separate. Too separate? Coach Paterno had immediately taken the matter to the highest levels of the university. It wasn't the coach or the athletic director who sought legal counsel on the matter. It was the highest administrative official at the university. It wasn't the coach or the athletic director who gave final approval to the course of action. It was the President of the university. What is Erickson talking about? From the words of Erickson and of the NCAA's Emmert, we know that words mean nothing in the world of American universities. The English language means nothing. Truth means nothing.

One member of the TV panel was Sara Ganim, a pleasant young reporter who, before she was twenty-five years old, brought a Pulitzer Prize to her newspaper for her early coverage of the Sandusky scandal. Does anyone doubt the power of this story when it brings a young woman the most prestigious prize in reporting? She found Penn State to be a frustrating place for a reporter. What kind of coach would close his practices? To her, Penn State was the Kremlin.

Bill Rhoden of the *New York Times* was there, spewing venom. So too was Buzz Bissinger, a slightly deranged-looking *Newsweek* contributor. The righteous Jim Rome, of ESPN fame, was also there. Sounding almost normal among this crew was CBS's own James Brown. But, of course, Brown wasn't logical either. He summed up the scandal as the football "tail wagging the dog." Did he have any clue as to who had been calling the shots?

Most panelists thought the NCAA penalties were appropriate, but Rhoden was livid because the football program hadn't been completely shut down. This humanitarian wanted NCAA actions that would punish the one hundred thousand fans who, every year, enjoy seven weekends of football in Happy Valley; and the tens of thousands more who watch the Nittany Lions on television. He wanted actions that would throw into disarray the lives of many young student athletes, and drive a stake into the economic hearts of scores of businesses in State College. Shutting down the football program would deny the Commonwealth of Pennsylvania the sales taxes, gasoline taxes, and beverage taxes paid by visitors attending games in State College. To what end?

Jim Rome said the Penn State officials had knowingly let a pedophile run free for years. Of course, that is the general belief. Rome and the American public are ready to believe that fate had brought together, at a single moment in time, five incredibly evil men.

To Buzz, Sandusky was part of the Penn State "football mafia." Is it that he didn't know, or didn't care, that Paterno and Sandusky had a very rocky professional relationship—and virtually no personal relationship? If this were politics, we Italian-Americans would have been offended by that one. For a moment, loopy Buzz went off message. He started to wonder why it took Corbett as Attorney General and, later, Governor, three years to charge a pedophile, when many thought he could have been charged immediately. We didn't get to see the reaction of the others when Buzz started to take them outside their comfort zone. Ganim could have picked up on this theme. From her reporting, she knew it had taken Corbett's investigators over two years after the initial complaint, which included allegations of oral sex, to search Sandusky's residence. But she knew that wasn't today's theme.

Buzz recovered. He had an inspiration. He told us that, running for office in Pennsylvania, Corbett had to be mindful of the Penn State community. Ah! That's better. The whole Penn State community would have punished a politician for indicting a pedophile. Buzz apparently didn't know or care that Corbett had received significant political contributions from officials at Sandusky's charity.

If the panel had included Franco Harris or anyone willing to defend the football program, it is likely the haters would have been asked what gave the NCAA jurisdiction and what evidence supported the punishment. No one on the panel asked how the football program led the president of the university to approve not reporting to the Department of Welfare.

There have been countless mindless attacks in the press. A recent example is Allen Barra's review of the new Paterno biography written by Joe Posnanski. Barra derides the book, and vilifies Paterno. The Freeh report makes the mistake of mashing the Penn State officials into one four-headed monster without examining the role and responsibilities of each. Barra sees only one monster, Paterno—he was the sole actor. The Freeh report, in the face of contrary evidence, provides a motive: the avoidance of bad publicity. This is too simplistic for Barra. He has a mind-reading skill that approaches the art of Michelangelo. Unlike the buffoon on *Face the Nation* who said Sandusky was part of the Penn State football mafia, Barra has learned from the book that Paterno and Sandusky did not like each other. So motivation becomes more complex. Follow this if you can:

Barra writes that Paterno "knew that Sandusky's brilliance as a defensive coordinator had been largely responsible for winning the two biggest games in Penn State history...the two games which gave Paterno his two national titles. Paterno knew that if Sandusky went down, it would take a piece of his reputation as well." Barra can see the wheels turning in Paterno's head: "If Sandusky goes down, my victory over Georgia is tarnished. If Sandusky goes down, my victory over Miami is tarnished. I can't let that happen."

So, with his reputation at stake, what does Paterno do when McQueary comes to him with the story of Sandusky in the shower with a boy? Does he say, "Mike, go home and shut up. No one need know about this"? Nope. Does he go to Curley the athletic director and say, "Tim, we got a problem with this McQueary guy; how are we going to contain it within the athletic department"? Nope. He sends McQueary not only to Curley but also to Schultz, the top administrative officer at the University. Schultz's domain includes human resources, internal auditing, and the campus police. Schultz brings in the President of the University. What? There goes the old ball game, and there goes the reputation. Oh, no. These guys are thinking of that Georgia game, and the Miami game, and they're saying, "We have to save Joe's reputation." Well, maybe not; maybe they had other motives. But it really doesn't matter in Barra's world. In that world, Paterno is omnipotent.

Barra can't even get his facts right. With great emotion, he asks, "If, God forbid, McQueary had been describing something that had been done to a member of Paterno's family, would he have been satisfied simply to contact Penn State's athletic director, put in him touch with McQueary, and walk away?" Of course, Paterno didn't simply contact the athletic director.

Before the Freeh report, two reporters crafted a book titled *Game Over Jerry Sandusky, Penn State and the Culture of Silence.* One author, investigative journalist Bill Moushey, had been nominated for a Pulitzer Prize. The other, Bob Dvorchak, is an award-winning reporter. Just as the title of my volume announces my point of view, so does the title of theirs.

The authors mention Paterno's closed practices. They document Paterno's well-known prickly relations with the press. They open one chapter with the words, "Penn State had a way of doing things in isolation." Apparently, from the book's title, all these things had something to do with the Sandusky scandal.

It's rather interesting, watching the reporters dance around the 1998 incident, where no charges were made against Sandusky. Just like the Frech report later, they try to excuse the authorities who failed to follow through on clues that Sandusky was a pedophile, while blaming Penn State officials for not doing enough. The writers question why Penn State didn't tell the world that Sandusky had been investigated and found innocent on a charge of molestation. They write, "In Happy Valley embarrassing secrets were kept under wraps." Are you kidding me? What was secret about an event that was investigated by the police, prosecutors, and the Department of Public Welfare? And what were the officials supposed to announce? As I have noted, in this case, clear thought is forever impossible.

In journalism there is no penalty for piling on. Apparently there is no penalty for trying to deceive, either.

ESPN commentator Mark May said on TV that Paterno and the other Penn State officials protected a child predator for at least 14 years. ESPN commentator Gene Wojciechowski echod May and added more. Here are a few of his Wojciechowski's nuggets;

> Paterno "lied through his teeth."
>
> Paterno's "silence from the first reported assault in 1998 helped empower a sexual predator for the next 13 years."
>
> "It can be reasonably argued he helped orchestrate a comprehensive cover-up...."
>
> Paterno had "the ability to stop a culture of concealment."
>
> "Paterno could have spoken out in 1998, but he didn't. He could have spoken out in 2001, but he didn't."
>
> "Paterno was an enabler."

"Orchestrate a comprehensive cover-up" is quite powerful, even if it is totally unsupported.The one concession the writer is willing to make regarding the 2001 incident is that Paterno "did the absolute minimum."

Perhaps we can't fault him for relying on the Freeh report. After all, as he is happy to tell us, the Freeh investigation included "more than 430 interviews and 3.5 million pieces of examined e-mails and documentation."

The gentle comment that Paterno "lied through his teeth" is based on the fact that Paterno told the grand jury he may have heard a rumor of the 1998 incident and the unlikely supposition that an e-mail disclosed that he was the coach that "is anxious to know." As has already been pointed out, the "coach" in this e-mail is almost certainly Sandusky. The e-mail that likely referred to Joe had the phrase "touched base," which is consistent with Paterno remembering a rumor eleven years later. But on this matter, Freeh fooled a lot of people.

In joining Freeh and the NCAA in condemning Paterno for keeping silent on the 1998 incident, Wojciechowski showed himself to be an irresponsible commentator. It should be obvious that it would have been utterly inappropriate for Paterno to have told the world that Sandusky had been suspected of child abuse after authorities had concluded there had been no abuse. This writer along with almost every other commentator, failed to note the absurdity in the Freeh report and in the NCAA's subsequent action.

Thus, he has no case related to 1998; and for 2001, he concedes that Paterno did the "absolute minimum." It serves my purpose here to grant that he occasionally used the English language correctly. I interpret "the absolute minimum" as meaning "he did nothing wrong."

Tell me again, Mr. Wojciechowski: after police, prosecutors, and welfare people found that Sandusky had done nothing wrong in 1998, and you reluctantly admit Paterno did nothing wrong in 2001, how did Joe Paterno enable a child molester?

The NCAA's haste in condemning Paterno was exceeded by the rush to judgment by the press. On July 15, 2012, three days after the Freeh report was released Tim Dahiberg of the Associated Press urged the NCAA to step in and punish Penn State. "There is no punishment," he wrote, "too severe for the cowardly lions." He wrote, "[T]he cult allowed to fester at Penn State has been exposed" and that "[T]he almighty football program at the center of all of this must pay." He also wrote that at Penn State, Paterno's "word was gospel." And he wrote this:

> Moral values went out the window when Paterno and the campus officials made no move to keep Sandusky off campus in 1998 after a woman complained her son had showered with the then-assistant coach. The pattern of deceit and dishonesty followed when no one turned Sandusky over to the police after he was seen sexually abusing a boy in the showers in the football locker room.

I know it gets a little repetitive, but let's go over this again. How is it that moral values "went out the window" when Penn State didn't fire an employee who was investigated but not charged? Penn State deceived no one about the 1998 incident, because it had been in the hands of the police, prosecutors, and welfare workers. With no deceit here, you can't have "a pattern of deceit." Dahiberg, like others, had been awed by Freeh's "independent investigation."

Dahiberg has no evidence that "the almighty football program" was "at the center of all of this." We can only pray that AP dispatches from around the world are held to a higher journalistic standard than this.

About the same time Dahiberg pronounced his judgment, Bob Costas, the respected NBC sports journalist was on TV's Face The Nation calling for Penn State to suspend its football program or for the NCAA to do it for them. Costas is relying on the Freeh report saying;

> "The Freeh report makes clear that in some sense he (Joe Paterno) was complicit, in some way he was among those who enabled Sandusky, not only to get away with what he had already done, but to continue to victimize other children."

Costas says Paterno's guilt is made "clear" by the Freeh report but when we look for the nature of that guilt we find he is guilty "in some sense", and complicit "in some way". We are left to wonder what Freeh made clear to Costas. By October, 2012, Costas was having second thoughts. On the Mike and Mike radio program Costas suggested that some of the Freeh report's strongest condemnations should perhaps be viewed more as conclusions than facts, and there may be some reexamination of these conclusions. Costas, unlike many, seems willing to reexamine his views.

Following the press treatment of the Sandusky scandal, we can easily understand Soren Kierkegaard when he wrote, "If Christ now came to earth, as sure as I live, He would not attack the high priests and the like: He would focus his attention upon the journalists."

After the Freeh report was released, Kevin Slaten, a tough-minded radio host on KFNS in St. Louis, who (unlike most) actually studied the report, had Christine Brennan from *USA Today* on his program to talk about Penn State. Brennan called the Freeh report "devastating" and "stunning in its volume." She called Paterno an enabler of a child rapist. Slaten tried to get Brennan to explain where in the Freeh report she had found evidence to support that outrageous charge. Her response was "all the e-mails." Hammered by Slaten to be more specific, she suddenly announced that she hadn't been told they were going to talk about the Freeh report. Slaten, not too gently, reminded her she had brought the Freeh report into the conversation. When Slaten pushed her to explain what Paterno should have done beyond bringing the McQueary account to the head of the campus police, she fell back on the canard that Paterno was the most powerful man on campus—and one of the most powerful men in Pennsylvania.

Slaten had found a perfect example of the journalists on the story: incapable of seeing the obvious flaws in the Freeh report, full of mindless emotion, lacking the ability to support their wild charges against Paterno. And so it goes.

Slaten was also was willing to take on a politician. University of Missouri football coach Gary Pinkel was one of the very few with the gumption to recall the good in Paterno's life, saying, "You can't erase all that this guy has done. You can't do that. Nobody can do that." State representative Sara Lampe, who was running for Lieutenant Governor, attacked Pinkel in what a press story called "a strongly worded statement." Pinkel had broken the new commandment—"Thou shall not speak well of Joe Paterno." Lampe asserted that "Coach Paterno protected and covered up for a serial child rapist and in doing so enabled him to keep raping children for another decade." Lampe then went on Slaten's radio program. Of course she couldn't support her wild charges, and she feebly announced she hadn't read the entire Freeh report.

It has been said that the more a person knows about the details of a matter reported in the press, the more the person knows the press got it wrong. That has been my experience. When I was with the Federal government I knew the details of numerous matters that received press coverage. I can think of only one instance where the press came close to getting it right, and in that instance they amused me with a little inaccuracy in the headline. I once ran an investigation into the practices of on-site inspections of Federal building construction projects. We found a number of deficiencies. One involved the testing of concrete. We observed that after samples were drawn for laboratory testing, more water was added to the concrete mix, making the lab results useless in determining the strength of the concrete actually laid.

The news article in a Washington DC paper got the facts about right, but the headline read, "GAO CHARGES SOUPY CEMENT." "Cement" is the dry stuff in a bag. When it is mixed with water and sand or gravel it becomes concrete. But "soupy concrete" doesn't have the nice alliterative ring of "soupy cement". Benjamin Disraeli once told Parliament, "Alliteration tickles the ear, and is a very popular form among savages." Many members of the press are nothing if they are not savages.

On October 10, 2012, Sandusky was sentenced to 30 to 60 years in prison. I will end the consideration of the press with an editorial in the New York Times of October 9, 2012, By now the press had had plenty of time to restudy the Freeh report. This prestigious newspaper opened its editorial with these words;

"The case of Jerry Sandusky over the serial raping of young boys while a coach in Penn State's football program ended Tuesday as it began, in denial and delusion."

The Times then enlightens us with this statement;

University officials, including head coach Joe Paterno looked the other way or covered up the crimes to protect a football program that brings in tens of millions of dollars a year."

The Times shares the widespread belief that disclosure of an ex-coaches activities, whatever they may have been, would have adversely affected Penn State football revenues. In what logic is this thought grounded? The story would have been that Penn State had reported an ex-coach as a suspected pedophile. The story that later emerged was that Penn State had covered up for a child rapist. Even then, there was no apparent drop in TV revenue and the drop in attendance was underway before the scandal broke. Penn State had significantly raised ticket prices for many of the seats in Beaver Stadium, and season ticket sales had declined. There is no evidence the scandal affected revenues other than then those lost because of the bowl sanctions imposed by the NCAA and no reason to believe a report in 2001 would have affected revenues or that the officials feared it would.

The Times refers to "crimes", apparently subscripting to the nonsense that the 1998 incident that had been investigated by the police and studied by prosecutors, had been "covered up" by Penn State. And of course the Times asserts that in 2001 Paterno knew Sandusky had committed a crime. On what evidence is that based?

In the editorial the Time's tells it readers;

"One of Sandusky's victims was a young boy who was sodomized by Mr. Sandusky in the Penn State football shower room, according to testimony by Mike McQueary, a former assistant coach. Mr. McQueary did nothing to stop the attack. He reported it the next day to Mr. Paterno who kept it from the police."

McQueary never testified that he saw sodomy and the jury found Sandusky not guilty of rape in the case of that victim. Upon these lies the Times then charges that Paterno "kept it from the police." Gentle reader, I'll bet your imagination is insufficient to allow you to write such a deliberate distortion. How in the world did Paterno keep it from the police? There wasn't a single individual who upon hearing McQueary's account believed the police should be notified. Beyond that, "kept it from the police" suggests an active role of suppression. Paterno's acts had no hint of suppression.

The Times then did the unthinkable. They pushed the new leadership at Penn State too far. The guys and gals at Penn State had rolled over for Mr. Freeh, they had rolled over for the NCAA, and their President had rolled over on Face the Nation, but when the Times charged them with denying "the obvious truth that football had been too dominant in Penn State's culture", the Penn State officials objected. They should have asked the Times to prove this "obvious truth" or where Freeh had proven this "obvious truth." That would have been fun. Instead Penn State President, Rodney Erickson responded with this;

> "As every member of the Penn State community knows, we are not defined by a single culture. We are a university whose cultures are rich and diverse, and are characterized by bold achievements in research, teaching and service, as well as athletics."

It wasn't much of a response, but it was something.

Mostly in this section I have been critical of sports journalists. But these are the people who ask such penetrating questions as "Coach, how important is it that your team has a lead at half-time." Here we are looking at the words of the New York Times.

There is no end to the nonsense an emotionally-packed story like the Sandusky scandal can generate. An article in the October 24th 2012, Washington Post leads with the headline- PENN STATE PROFESSOR SUES THINK TANK, MAGAZINE. The article, concerning a law suit filed by Professor Michael Mann, opens with this paragraph;

"A Nobel Peace Prize winner and Penn State University climate science professor has sued a Washington-based think tank and a national magazine that called his scientific findings fraudulent and compared him to Jerry Sandusky, the former Penn State football coach convicted of numerous counts of child molestation."

According to the article;

"The lawsuit is based on a July 13 article by Rand Simberg published on the Competitive Enterprise Institute's blog, titled "The Other Scandal in Unhappy Valley". It followed an investigation this summer that said some Penn State officials knew of Sandusky's sexual abuse of minors before he was arrested and chose not to report them to authorities."

"The article compared Sandusky to Mann, accusing the the (sic) scientist of "molesting data" about global warming. It was later summarized and linked to by the National Review. In that piece National Review writer Mark Steyn says "Not sure I'd have extended that metaphor all the way into the locker-room showers with quite the zeal Mr. Simberg does. But he has a point.""

I guess the courts will decide what kind of point Mr. Simberg had.

There were a couple of points about the treatment of the Sandusky scandal in this article that interested me. Unlike most articles this one does not mention "rape." It uses the more general phrase, "sexual abuse of minors." Also it does not mention "cover up" or the police. It accurately says the officials "chose not to report them to authorities." It seems the press can get it right except when they deliberately choose to be sensational.

15

Disbar Freeh—Reform The National Collegiate Avengers Association (NCAA)

The most saddening thing about the NCAA's actions is that they were taken with undue haste. The Roman, Publilius Syrus, wrote, "Haste in giving judgment is criminal." I agree.. If the NCAA has chosen to become a moral force in America, sweeping across college campuses in its Batmobile and finding and punishing actions it deems to be moral transgressions, it must change its name and bylaws. The National Collegiate Avengers Association would be an appropriate name. New bylaws should define the scope of its jurisdiction and institute due process into its proceedings. We know the law says they need not employ due process, but I am sure the esteemed men and women who lead our most prestigious universities will, on reflection, see that it's the right thing to do.

I know nothing of the professional standards for lawyers. I'm not even sure that isn't an oxymoron. But shouldn't deliberately and continually lying to a client subject an attorney to severe discipline?

In my opinion, when Freeh told his client he found evidence of an unhealthy "culture of reverence for the football program that is ingrained at all levels of the campus community," he lied.

When Freeh told his clients that when Sandusky retired, the Penn State officials had reason to believe he was "a suspected child predator," he lied.

I believe when Freeh found four officials equally guilty of any and all alleged failures, he lied.

When Freeh claimed to have proof the men concealed facts to avoid bad publicity, he lied.

I think the Freeh report is replete with lies, large and small. Is there no day of reckoning?

I will end where I began. Policemen, welfare workers, prosecutors, janitors, officials of a charity run for children, the president of a university, a medical doctor, a graduate assistant, and the graduate student's father all failed to bring Sandusky to justice. An Attorney General sat on evidence of Sandusky's child abuse and dithered. All get a free pass. Only Joe Paterno, with less knowledge then any of them and less authority than most of them, gets crucified by a "remember-the-children" press. There have been accounts of Paterno saying, "I wish I had done more." Some have taken this as a confession. The full quote is "With the benefit of hindsight, I wish I had done more." That is quite a different thing.

To the last days of life, Joe Paterno was a man of honor. He lived by the rules, and he played by the rules. It was not dishonorable to believe that the highest officials of a prestigious university would do the right thing on a sensitive matter.

Here is my opinion on who were dishonorable. The prosecutors who, without evidence, told the world that a graduate assistant had seen a boy raped in a Penn State shower and had reported the rape to Joe Paterno were dishonorable. The members of the Penn State Board of Trustees who fired Paterno because of clamors from the press were dishonorable. The university presidents, responding to the same clamors, who voted to punish Paterno and his program without proper study, were dishonorable.

And then there are the members of the press. This is a group with a strange sense of honor. If one of their members steals someone's words, that's plagiarism, and that is severely punished. But if they steal someone's honor, that's simply business as usual. They live for the sensational story, and they don't let facts get in the way. And if, from their perch above mere mortals, they can cast themselves as the great free press rooting out evil, all the better.

And what is one to say of Louis Freeh? His lies and distortions were cold, calculated, and deliberate.

I know where Joe Paterno is in the afterlife. St. Peter will have to decide on the others.

Epilogue

The Freeh Key Findings

A Sampler

When I did audit and investigative work, a "finding" comported to the dictionary definition:

Finding *n.* The results or conclusions of an investigation.

A finding was not a simple statement of a mundane fact. It was not an editorial or an invitation to the reader to draw an unwarranted conclusion. Each chapter of the Freeh report is led by a "Key Findings" section. Here's a very small sample:

> Sandusky was convicted of several assaults that occurred after the 1998 incident. Some of those sexual assaults against young boys might have been prevented had Sandusky been prohibited from bringing minors to University facilities and University bowl game.

Comment:

> *The 1998 incident was the one where, after an investigation that included the police, prosecutors, and the Department*

of Public Welfare, Sandusky had been cleared of all charges. If the authorities had done their job, Sandusky would have been prevented from any further sexual assaults. How do you blame the Penn State officials?

Curley talked with Sandusky about his future role with the football program and offered him the possibility of an Assistant Athletic Director Position.

Comment:

I'm still trying to figure out what is "key" about this statement. The report has a number of "key findings" of similar gravity.

On Friday, February 9, 2001, University graduate assistant Michael McQueary observed Sandusky involved in sexual activity with a boy in the coach's shower room in the University's Lasch Building. McQueary met with and reported the incident to Paterno on Saturday, February 10, 2001. Paterno did not immediately report what McQueary told him, explaining that he did not want to interfere with anyone's weekend.

Comment:

The Freeh investigators never established what McQueary saw or reported. The medical doctor who was one of the first to hear McQueary's account has stated that McQueary denied seeing anything sexual.

Despite an expressed reluctance to "interfere with anyone's weekend," Paterno did just that. He met with Schultz and Curley the next day, a Sunday. How immediately did Freeh want Paterno to report?

On February 26, 2001, Schultz e-mailed Curley, confirming the plan from the prior day's meeting. This e-mail and several that follow are written in unusually cryptic tones, without the use of proper names or titles.

Comment

Wow! The investigators got something here. Writing in code! Well, at least "unusually cryptic tones." "Unusual" to whom, we wonder?

Luckily our crack codebreakers were on the job. In truth, no one would have any problem understanding the e-mails. Freeh leaves out the damning evidence that the e-mails weren't signed, "Sincerely yours."

On September 21, 2001, Schultz obtained Board approval for the sale of a parcel of Penn State land to The Second Mile. The Board minutes do not reflect any contemporaneous discussion of the 2001 investigation, the propriety of a continuing relationship between Penn State and The Second Mile, or the risks involved by allowing Sandusky to be prominently associated with Penn State. Schultz even issued a press release about the transaction lauding Sandusky.

Comment:

Where do you begin with this one? Those damn Penn State officials, not only are they covering up for a pedophile, they are doing public business with him, or more precisely, with his organization. I am not sure what we are to infer from this. This transaction seems to me to demonstrate how benignly the McQueary report was viewed. We wonder what attorney Freeh thinks of Governor Corbett approving a multimillion dollar grant to The Second Mile during a time the Governor knew Sandusky was being investigated, after serious charges of child sexual abuse had been lodged against him.

The NCAA cited the Freeh report as supporting the sanctions it imposed on the football program. Rather than go through the entire report, let's look at the "Key Findings" segments. Surely we will find support for the NCAA sanctions there. Following are the chapters with key findings.

Chapter 1. The Pennsylvania State University—Governance and Administration

There are five key findings. The only one remotely related to the football program is this:

The Department of Intercollegiate Athletics ("Athletic Department") involving approximately 800 student-athletes, has an Associate Athletic Director responsible for approximately 800 student-athletes, has an Associate Athletic Director responsible for compliance and was significantly understaffed.

Chapter 2. Response of University Officials to the Allegation of Child Sexual Abuse Against Sandusky—1998

There are ten key findings. One relates to the football program:

Before May 1998, several staff members and football coaches regularly observed Sandusky showering with young boys in the Lasch Building (now the East Area Locker Building or "Old Lasch"). None of the individuals interviewed notified their superiors of this behavior.

Chapter 3. Sandusky's Retirement from the University—1999

It's hard to understand the attention devoted to Sandusky's retirement. He seems to have received very favorable terms, but it is unclear what is to be inferred about the football program from the seven key findings.

Chapter 4. Response of University Officials to the Allegation of Child Sexual Abuse Against Sandusky—2001

There are 23 "Key Findings" in this important chapter.

One finding asserts that janitors, knowing of a sexual assault by Sandusky in a football shower room on a young boy, failed to report it because they feared they "would be fired." Here the fear is not explained. In the body of the report, a janitor helpfully explains it was Paterno they feared.

Freeh may want the reader to associate all the actions of the Penn State officials described in this Chapter with the "football culture," but that is an unstated backdrop. None of the "findings" involving the Penn State officials describe, or even suggest, any football culture influence.

Chapter 5. Response of University Officials to the Grand Jury Investigation—2010, 2011

None of the thirteen key findings in this section have any relevance to the actions of the Penn State officials in 2001.

Chapter 6. Board of Trustees

Freeh makes no attempt to link any of the eight key findings in this section to the football program.

Chapter 7. Sandusky's Post-Retirement Interactions with the University

The seven key findings express Freeh's disapproval of the University's respectful treatment of Sandusky and his charity after reports of possible sexual misconduct. There is no attempt to directly link this treatment to the football culture.

Chapter 8. Federal and State Child Sexual Abuse Reporting Requirements

There are six key findings for this chapter. Most are versions of the theme that "awareness and interest in Clery Act compliance throughout the University remained significantly lacking."

More relevant to the investigation, the one key finding points out that "Campus Security Authorities" must report crimes to the police. Under the law, athletic directors and coaches are "Campus Security Authorities." It would seem logical that even without this law, crimes should be reported to the police.

The relevant key finding states:

Paterno, Curley and McQueary were obligated to report the 2001 Sandusky incident to the University Police Department for inclusion in Clery Act statistics and for determining whether a timely warning should be issued to the University community.

Is that why they should have reported it? Logic is not a strong point of the Freeh investigators. The issue of what should have been reported, and to whom, is central to the entire investigation. It should not be obliquely addressed with reference to the Clery Act.

It would be interesting to know if the attorney who advised Schultz on "reporting of suspected child abuse" mentioned the Clery Act. But like so much after the Freeh investigation, we just don't know. And remember, neither McQueary's father nor the medical doctor thought reporting to the police was appropriate.

Chapter 9. The Protection of Children in University Facilities and Programs
The four findings here highlight weaknesses that could have allowed workers and volunteers to interact with children in the University's youth programs without proper background checks. These weaknesses did not grow from the football culture.

The Freeh report lists eighty-three key findings. Which ones persuaded the NCAA that it had the right to sanction the university?

If Paterno failed to do the right thing (an assertion I strongly reject), it was the failure of an individual, not of a program, and the NCAA has no basis to ascribe a football motive. Freeh's conclusions are irresponsible, and the NCAA's actions are disgraceful.

There are some in the Penn State nation who believe the NCAA will see the error of its way and correct the injustice. I am not among them. I have observed human nature over many years. It is my experience that the average person may admit to a mistake; when faced with overwhelming evidence or feeling remorse, a person may even admit to a crime. It is my experience that the influential and powerful rarely admit mistakes or show remorse. We may find that Bob Costas is an exception. Paterno was an exception when he said, "With the benefit of hindsight, I wish I had done more." The august body of university presidents that could reduce the sanctions and restore Joe Paterno's hard-earned and well-deserved victories will not. Why should we expect a showing of character and decency from these people now?

Acknowledgments

I want to thank Eileen Morgan and John Ziegler, for getting out there early with spirited defenses of Joe Paterno. Franco Harris has been a strong supporter of Paterno and his program. As a public figure, he knew he would be the subject of mindless scorn for defending the Penn State program, and of course he was.

I am not in the listening range of Kevin Slaten, but I have heard no radio show hosts in the Washington D.C. area with the knowledge or the gumption to take on the Freeh report as he has.

My goal has been to reach those who do not spend their time on the Internet. This work began as a magazine article. I quickly realized there are few national magazines available for a story like this. The two that I tried had no interest. Perhaps the *Atlantic Monthly* was uninterested because my writing did not meet their editorial standards. I had sent them an article. That could not have been the case with *Mother Jones.* I had sent them only a query. My writing is not very elegant, but I suspect it was my point of view, not my lack of writing skills, that led to their lack of interest in a story of great national interest.

Sources

The principle sources for this work can be found on the Internet. The best way to find an article is to use key words. These should bring you to the site addresses listed below and possibly others.

THE FREEH REPORT
    www.thefreehreportonpsu.com/REPORT_FINAL
THE SANDUSKY PRESENTMENT
    attorneygeneral.gov../Sandusky-grandjury-presentment/\
NCAA ON PENN STATE SANCTIONS
    http://www.politicolnews.com/penn-state-ncaa-sanctions-too-big-to-fail/
    http://Onlineathens.com/sports/college-sports/2012-07-24/ncaa=president-emmert-hopes-
CORBETT-"REMEMBER THE CHILDREN"
    espn.go.com/espn/otl/story/ /id7770966/in-wake-joe-paterno-death-sandusky-sex-..
VAN NATTA ON CORBETT
    http://espn.go.com/espn/otl/story/_id/7770996/in-wake-joe-paterno-death-sandusky-sex-...

TRANSCRIPT: JOE PATERNO'S GRAND JURY TESTIMONY
Http:sportsbybrooks.co/transcript-joe-paterno-grand-jury-tes-timony-29933

STATE SENATOR LAMPE ON COACH PINKEL
http:/www.kansascity.com/2012/07/19/3713348/state-repre-sentive-chastises.html

NEW YORK TIMES EDITORIAL ON SANDUSKY VERDICT
http://www.nytimes.com/2012/10/1opinion/the-sandusky-rape-verdict.htmnl

WASHINGTON POST EDITORIAL ON NCAA PENN STATE SANCTIONS
http.//www.morning/journal.com/articles/2012/2/07/25/opinion/doc500f6d34c9c9309903210.

SALLY JENKINS "PATERNO IS A LIAR"
www.washingtonpost.com/..paterno../glJQAMUXA/9fW.story.html

SALLY JENKIN'S INTERVIEW WITH PATERNO
www..washingtonpost.com/..paterno../interview../glQA08.elyp_stor

PATERNO "BENEFIT OF HINDSIGHT"
Deadspin.com/..joe-paterno-statement-with-thebenefit-of-hindsight

PSU PROFESSORS ON "CULTURE"
www.centredaily.com/2012/09/../study-counter-tripon-claims

ALLEN BARRA PATERNO BOOK REVIEW
http://www.theatlantic.com/entertainment/archive/2012/08/paterno-a-relentless-failed-defe..

ALLEGED SANDUSKY VICTIM 2
http://deadspin.com/5952297/sanduskys-undentified-shower-victim-not-unidentified-say..

TIM DAHIBERG ON NCAA AND PENN STATE
http://chronicle.northcoastnow.com/2012/07/15tim-dahlberg-ncaa-has-to-punish-penn-stat

EILEEN MORGAN PENN STATE ADVERTISEMENT
http://notpsu.blogspot.com/2012/08/eileen-morgan-full-page-adletter.html

Sources

EILEEN MORGAN THE REAL FACTS ABOUT JOE PATERNO AND PSU

www.emf.inthough.net

DR. DRANOV TESTIMONY

http://blogspot.com/2012/09/dr-dranovs-testimony-transcript.html

THE 2011 ACADEMIC BOWL CHAPIONSHIP

http://higheredwach.newamerica.net/blogposts/2011/2011_abcsranking-6-200

MICHAEL MCCANN ON FREEH REPORT

http://sportsillustrated.cnn.com/2012/writers/michael_mccann/07/12/freeh-report-penn-stat..

MICHAEL MCCANN ON SANDUSKY TRIAL

http://sportsillustgrated.cnn.com/2012/writers/michael-mccann/06/20/jerry-sandusky-trial-d..

GENE WOJCIECHOWSKI JOE PATERNO ENABLER

http://espn.go.com/college-football/story/_/id81604/30/college-football-joe-paterno-enable..

BOB COSTAS CALL FOR SHUT DOWN PENN STATE PROGRAM

http://bleacherreport.com/articles/1261684-bob-costas-calls-for-penn-state-to-shut-down

JOHN ZIEGLER'S SITE

www.framingpaterno.com has links to many articles related to the Freeh report and the Sandusky scandal.

Addendum

For the media, the Sandusky scandal is the gift that keeps on giving. On November 1, 2012, as this book was being prepared for printing, additional charges were filed against two Penn State officials who had already been criminally charged for matters related to the scandal and, for the first time, charges were filed against the former President of Penn State University, Graham Spanier.

At a press conference, Pennsylvania Attorney General Linda Kelly and Frank Noonan, Commissioner, Pennsylvania State Police, announced new criminal charges related to the Sandusky scandal. Tim Curley and Gary Schultz who were facing charges of perjury and failure to report are now charged with endangering the welfare of children, criminal conspiracy, and obstruction of justice. Graham Spanier, who had not been previously charged, now faces the same charges as the other two officials.

Kelly told the press;

> "It was the activity in those football locker rooms first reported by a victim in 1998 and again by a witness in 2002, (sic) that are particularly disturbing. The incident which occurred in 2002 (sic) in Lash Hall (sic) where Sandusky

was seen committing a sexual assault on a young boy of about 10 years of age was reported to University officials by a graduate assistant who happened to be in the building late one Friday evening."

Taking a page from the Freeh report Kelly told the press the officials "never made any attempt to identify that child." [3] This ignores the fact that the Penn State officials reported the matter to Sandusky's charity, an organization with a duty to identify the child.

Kelly is eloquent on the importance of truthful reporting under oath to a Grand Jury saying;

> "I'd like to emphasize that one of the basic principles of our legal system is that witnesses are required under the law to tell the truth when they are called before a Grand Jury. The truth, pure and simple, nothing more, nothing less. And that principle applies to everyone from the ordinary man on the street as well as to those who occupy positions of power and influence, men like the defendants in this case."

Alright Ms. Kelly, we know you extend that basic principle to powerful men before a Grand Jury trying to recount events of a decade earlier. How about members of the police testifying under oath in a criminal trial about events that occurred within the year, and events that occurred moments before? Apparently your sacred principle doesn't apply to them.

During the Sandusky trial, defense attorneys were trying to establish the fact that the police had possibly tainted the accounts given by accusers by informing them of other accusers.

> Reporter Sarah Ganim gave this account of an event on one day of the Sandusky trial;
> "Two of the lead investigators in the Sandusky case took the stand several times this morning and answered

---

[3] Kelly made a plea for boy in the shower to come forward. Apparently it has been determined that the young man claiming to be Victim 2 is not Victim 2.

differently under oath when asked if they had been discussing testimony in the courthouse hallways.

"State Police Trooper Scott Rossman and retired trooper Joseph Leiter both testified several times about a tape-recording made during the police interview with the 28-year old known as Victim 4. And when they were called to the stand for the last time, defense attorney Karl Rominger asked them both if they had discussed Lieter's testimony in the courthouse corridors. Rossman replied that they did not. Leiter, when asked the same question, said they did.

"The recording had been played by the defense to show that contrary to Leiter's first testimony on the stand, he did share with victim 4 how many other accusers there were, and what they had said in interviews with police.

"In the recording, while victim 4 was taking a smoke break, his civil attorney can be heard whispering to Leiter with suggestions on how to get him to open up.

"Can we at some point in time say to him, 'Listen, we've interviewed other kids, and other kids have told us that there was intercourse and they admitted, you know, is there anything else you want to tell us?'"

It seems Lieter was happy to oblige. When the victim returned to the room, Lieter told him nine other victims were interviewed and talked about abuse. The tape of this exchange had been played to the jury. On the stand Lieter couldn't remember having mentioned any number of other accusers.

During the press conference, Commissioner Noonan mentioned the police investigation of 1998 when "nothing happened" and, according to Noonan, "nothing happened" in 2000, when janitors saw a sex act in the shower and didn't report it because they "were afraid of their jobs", and then the graduate assistant saw a sex act, and "nothing happened." Apparently Noonan believes the Penn State officials are responsible in all these cases; not only when the graduate assistant reported something, but also when the police investigated and the District Attorney was involved and no charges were brought, and when the janitors saw something and said nothing.

Commonwealth authorities again asserted that the graduate assistant saw and reported a sex act. In the new Grand Jury Presentment they obliquely deal with the fact that Dr. Dranov, a family friend, had heard one of graduate assistant McQueary's first accounts and had testified he was never told that McQueary had seen a sex act. According to the recent Presentment "Michael McQueary relayed some of what he had observed to his father and Dr. Dranov." Then, according to the Presentment, the next day McQueary "reported to Paterno what he had witnessed between Sandusky and the boy the night before." The prosecutors want us to believe that McQueary gave Paterno a full description of what he had seen, but had told his father and Dr Dranov, only "some of what he had observed." Does this sound reasonable? I think they got it backward, and not by accident.

In making the new charges against the three Penn State officials the Presentment states;

> "The plan of action undertaken by these three administrators, who formed the very apex of decision making and power at Penn State was created out of a desire to shield Sandusky from the criminal process and, perhaps most importantly, to spare the University tremendous negative publicity and embarrassment."

Oh my goodness. The media had me convinced that all the power at Penn State resided with Joe Paterno. I didn't know about this apex of power.

Reading the Presentment I could not tell what acts by the officials beyond those related to the previous charges of "failure to report" represented "endangering the welfare of children." So it was impossible for me to understand why this charge was made, and why it was made now rather than before.

After the press conference Spanier's attorneys fired back with their own statement calling the Presentment a farce and saying;

> "Today's Presentment is the latest desperate act by Governor Tom Corbett to cover up and divert attention

away from the fact that he failed to warn the Penn State community about the suspicions surrounding Jerry Sandusky and instead knowingly allowed a child predator to roam free in Pennsylvania. Its timing speaks volumes."

According to the attorneys;

"There is no factual basis to support these charges which may explain why the Attorney General and her staff refused to meet with Dr. Spanier or his lawyers to discuss the matter despite repeated attempts to do so, or to accept Dr. Spanier's offer to appear before the Grand Jury again to clarify any misconceptions."

The Governor's press secretary returned fire, calling the statement "the ranting of a man who has just been indicted for covering up for a convicted pedophile." It is clear the courts will be busy for a while.

This latest swirl of emotion-packed charges again gives us a reminder of how the scandal has made clear thought impossible. I have always respected Jeffrey Toobin, author and CNN legal commentator. To me he had always seemed knowledgeable and sensible. After the Kelly/Noonan press conference Toobin said "This has to rank as one of the most shocking and appalling stories that I have ever encountered." "Year after year", Toobin said, "the cops are not informed and this guy continues to be in contact with children." The cops were informed in 1998, Jeffrey, did you forget that?

Toobin then says that the Penn State officials learned that Sandusky was "sexually assaulting – and that's what it was –a child in the showers of a football stadium. . ." Toobin has no doubt "that's what it was." Where does this certainty come from? Another legal analyst, Michael McCann. was not so certain McQueary had seen and reported a sexual assault. Toobin continues;

"Where were the police? Where were the authorities? And again, I'm not blaming the authorities. Why was no one calling them when all these things were coming out year after year?"

Holy God in heaven! What is this man talking about? All what things coming out year after year? There was one year, with one incident known by Penn State officials, where the authorities were not called in. Toobin is not blaming the authorities? Why not? Not blaming the police, the prosecutors and the welfare workers who refused to adequately investigate Sandusky in 1998 when they had every reason to do so? Toobin is not so forgiving when the Penn State officials were involved, and he is not so forgiving when it comes to Joe Paterno. He acknowledges that he saw no evidence of a criminal act by Paterno but he then says;

> "Given the magnitude of these allegations, given the, you know, seriousness, the fact that all he did was make one meeting with the athletic director and didn't take steps to see the police were involved and didn't take steps to see Jerry Sandusky banned from the Penn State campus, I mean is really shocking."

Here we go again. Paterno is not involved in these latest charges, but Toobin has to take a swing at him. And he can't get the facts right. Paterno didn't just go to the athletic director and dump it in his lap. At the same time he went to the highest administrative official at Penn State, a man whose responsibilities included the campus police. Twice Paterno followed up with the witness inviting a suggestion if more should have been done. Toobin refers to "the magnitude of these allegations". That's a strong phrase when it is unclear just what McQueary reported. Is there nowhere for the public to turn to get honest reporting?

On November 10, 2012, Franco Harris and his wife, Dana, held a Town Hall meeting in Pittsburgh with the theme *Upon further Review: Penn State one year later.* Eileen Morgan and Ray Blehar made presentations detailing errors and distortions in segments of the Freeh report. John Zeigler showed portions of a documentary he is developing on the framing of Paterno. There was a panel discussion. One of the panelists was Bob Dvorchak, co-author of the book, *Game Over: Jerry Sandusky, Penn State and the Culture of Silence.* I had an opportunity to ask Dvorchak how he could link Paterno's closed practices and other examples of poor press relations with the criminal act of covering up a crime. His answer was, in effect, that

CPSIA information can be obtained at www.ICGtesting.com
Printed in the USA
LVOW072331240213

321506LV00008B/160/P

the latter was a natural outgrowth of the former. When I responded that I rejected that argument, the audience applauded. This was a pro-Paterno crowd. Unfortunately many are willing to make the absurd connection.

Also on the panel was Rob Tribeck, counsel to the organization *Penn State for Responsible Stewardship* (PS4RS), an organization dedicated to having the Board of Trustee members who supported the ouster of Paterno replaced with new members; is encouraging calls for a new investigation; and seeks to provide support for Sandusky's victims and others negatively impacted by the scandal. Tribeck is an attorney who has managed to combine a passionate support of Joe Paterno with a cold objectivity. The group has looked critically at the Freeh report.

In November, 2012, the group released an examination of Freeh's assertion that Penn State could have, and should have, restricted Sandusky's access after the 1998 incident. PS4RS wrote that, under Pennsylvania law, after an investigation into alleged child sexual abuse had concluded that no charges should be brought, but child abuse was "indicated", there would have been steps available for Penn State to take some action regarding an employee. But the investigation of 1998 did not include the finding that abuse had been "indicated". According to PS4RS;

> "As a result, and contrary to the suggestions of the Freeh Report and the NCAA, not only would it have been improper for Penn State, or any individual at Penn State, to take negative action against Jerry Sandusky in 1998, it would have been illegal under the law. "Thus, irrespective of the knowledge of the 1998 incident by Penn State, or any individual at Penn State, no negative action against Sandusky would have been permitted.
>
> "Accordingly, the suggestion, within the Freeh Report, subsequently adopted by the NCAA, that Penn State was somehow responsible for a lack of action in 1998 is simply false. Such a suggestion is reckless at best and, at worst, represents a deliberate attempt to mislead."

It seems every attack on Paterno is reckless at best and, at worst, represents a deliberate attempt to mislead.